COOKING UNDER PRESSURE

THE ULTIMATE GUIDE & RECIPE COOKBOOK FOR ELECTRIC PRESSURE COOKERS

By Joel C. Brothers

Acknowledgements

When the publishing company told me the book they had contracted with me to write was about pressure cookers, I was somewhat less than enthusiastic. After all, I am a professional chef, and chefs never use pressure cookers. They are what grandmother's cook in, right? I am pleased to say that I was never more wrong. Not only do pressure cookers retain the most flavor and nutrients in your food, but the modern models, especially the electric ones, are some of the easiest appliances to use. And I was really impressed by the safety features. We've come a long way from when my grandmother used to enlist our help with the canning chores. Modern pressure cookers are a serious culinary tool, and no kitchen should be without one. While developing recipes for this book, I learned just how versatile a tool a pressure cooker can be. And how convenient, as well. I was sent a Wolfgang Puck 6 QT. Bistro Elite pressure cooker to use for this project, and I put it through every conceivable test, including breaking and repairing the handle, and allowing the seal to seat improperly and let the water steam out. The unit passed all tests with flying colors, and is still operating nicely. About the only thing I didn't do was drop it from an airplane, or tall building. I am now convinced that good quality modern pressure cookers are a wise investment. I would like to thank the Customer Service, and Technical Support people at Wolfgang Pucks company for all their help and advice. I'd also like to thank the people at the Home Shopping Network for sending me the pressure cooker, which they have allowed me to keep. Special thanks to the great people at Presto International for their invaluable information on design, science and the history of pressure cookers. And most of all, my sincerest thanks to my loving wife, Sue. Without her assistance with proof-reading and editing, suggestions, and support, this book would not have been possible. And lastly, my sincerest thanks to my neighbors, who helped us eat all the left-overs when the refrigerator got too full. I hope you enjoy using this book as much as I did writing it.

Sincerely. Joel C. Brothers

PS. – New 2016 update

We have received an Instant Pot IP-DUO60 7-in-1 Multi-Functional Pressure cooker, 6Qt/1000W, 7-in-1 Multi-Functional Cooker—Pressure Cooker, Slow Cooker, Rice Cooker, Sauté/Browning, Yogurt Maker, Steamer & Warmer. It is an amazing cooking machine and we are using it every day to develop new recipes and new ways to use it. We will be publishing a recipe book and guide for the Instant Pot in the near future. We did however add a small section in this book to help you use our recipes using the Instant Pot.

We have also added 75 additional new recipes for 2016 and have updated several others.

We are also publishing a new book of Electric Pressure Cooker fan favorites. All the recipes in the book will be recipes sent to us and tested by us. All participants will get full credit for their recipes if picked and a link to their site or blog. If you would like to participate email us at electricpressurecooking@gmail.com

Table of Contents

PART ONE

Basic Principles

Introduction to Pressure Cooking

Cooking today is not like it was even just 20 or 30 years ago. With single-parent families on the rise, both parents working, and everybody seemingly on the way to, or from somewhere, all the time, it has become much harder to function as a home-maker, whether you're a mom, or a dad. With so little time, many families exist, for the most part, on fast-foods, and pre-packaged, heavily processed foods with dubious nutritional value. Don't get me wrong. I am not painting the commercial food companies as villains. They are doing an outstanding job in providing the world with a usable food supply, but there are limits as to what can be done to food, and still have it be as nutritious as it should be. Everything is a trade-off. For instance, most of the nutrition in a wheat kernel is contained in the oils and the bran. In fact, over 70 important vitamins and other nutrients are all contained within the oils and bran. But, once the grain is ground into flour, these oils, vitamins, and nutrients quickly oxidize, rendering them unusable within as little as 48 hours. And the oils will quickly break down and go rancid. So, in order for flour to be able to sit on a grocery store shelf, and in your pantry without going bad, these oils have to be removed. So all you are getting in a bag of flour is the endosperm part of the kernel, which is all starch, and little usable nutrients. To fight nutritional deficiencies like pellagra, and beriberi, food companies have to add some vitamins back into the flour from other sources, namely 14 vitamins and minerals that are essential to the body. This is what they mean when they say it is 'Fortified'. Any time you see this word on food, it means that the finished product did not have enough nutrition left in it to sustain life, and they had to add some back to it. So, they remove 70 nutrients, and replace 14, all so you can buy a bag of flour and keep it on your shelf for a few weeks. We're trading nutrition for convenience, because that's what consumers want.

Is it a problem? Well, yes, and no. Most people do not eat just bread, and can get these other nutrients from other sources. But there are a lot of nutrients in food that react with each other, and affect things like our immune systems, and we just don't completely understand how they work. We know that people who eat whole, fresh grains have healthier immune systems, and are able to maintain a healthy weight much easier, but we don't know exactly why. This is just one of many examples.

Especially in the US, our population, on average, is over-weight, and we have an increased level of weight and nutritionally-associated health problems, such as heart disease, diabetes, etc... Even some cancers are suspected to be linked, at least partially, to nutrition. Food additives, used to preserve food longer on the shelf, or enhance the flavor (such as lots of added sugar and salt) directly contribute to these health issues. We've been making these trade-offs for so long that we seem to be unable to determine a 'break-even' point. At what level do the health risks outweigh the importance of convenience? At the present time, an individual must make that decision on their own.

But even if you do decide that the risks are too great, what can you do? Most people do not have the time, knowledge, or facilities to make most of their own flour, cornmeal, bread, or make things from scratch, like catsup (to avoid the high fructose corn syrup used in making it....a major contributor to diabetes...), mustard, and other things. Normally, dried beans take a lot of planning, such as overnight soaking, and take hours to cook. Unless you want to feed your family at midnight, that makes cooking them when you get home from your job, an unworkable proposition.

Who would have ever thought that a 500 year-old invention could save the situation? A long time ago (1649 AD...), a thoughtful mathematician and physicist came up with a way to preserve most of the nutrients in food, and allow it to be transported great distances, feed ships crews, transport food to the needy in remote areas of the world, and in the early 18th century it was even used to feed Napoleons army. During the Great Depression, it was used to get the most nutrition out of the available foods, and even to be able to eat some things that normally would be too tough to be edible. During WW-II, it was used to speed up cooking times for women working in Defense plants, and to get the most out of their rationed foods. The answer, it would seem, has been around even before the problem existed.

I am speaking of the humble pressure cooker. Although it has gone through several evolutions in the last 500 years, it still operates on the same basic principles as Papin's original 'Digester'. That is to say, super-heated steam is used under pressure to drive in nutrients and flavor, rather than leach it out or destroy it, as in other cooking methods. Through a simple application of a few basic Laws of Physics, most of the available nutrition in food can be retained, as well as significantly shortening the cooking time. With a modern pressure cooker, entire meals, even dried beans, can be prepared in an hour, or less. Whole grains can be cooked in minutes, instead of hours, and food can even be canned at home, with complete quality-control, for future use. It is possible to break the cycle of huge amounts of salts, sugars, preservatives and other additives that may be effecting you, and you family's health adversely.

There are a host of advantages to using a modern pressure cooker:

- Speed-as a rule, most foods will cook in a third of the time in a pressure cooker. Some, even faster.

- More nutrition-pressure cooking is the #1 way to preserve the most nutrients in your food, other than eating them raw. It retains the most nutrients of any other cooking method there is.

- Convenience-most modern electric pressure cookers can be safely loaded, turned on, and left to cook while you are at work. They have digital electronics that monitor the food, keep it warm for as long as two days, and will stop cooking when the food is done, or if there are any safety issues, all automatically. Dinner can be ready as soon as everyone gets home.

- Safety-frozen foods can be easily cooked without thawing them out, making it much safer, especially for fast spoiling foods like fish, seafood and poultry. All modern pressure cookers have redundant safety features for over-pressure, under pressure, and will not let you open the lid if there is pressure in the unit. They are as safe as cooking gets.

- Better health-pressure cooked food do not require a lot of oils, fats, and spices to cook. You can reduce them to almost nothing, and enjoy the natural taste of the food itself. This results in fewer bad calories, lower cholesterol, less sugar and salt, etc....

- Ease of use-pressure cookers are so easy to use that anyone, regardless of what level of culinary talent they have (if any at all...) can successfully use a modern pressure cooker. Even children can quickly master the basic principles involved (but children should always be supervised when doing anything in the kitchen...even dishes and sweeping...). Cooking doesn't get any easier than this. It's as fool-proof as cooking gets.

There are probably a lot of other advantages as well. You're really only limited by your imagination. In the following pages, you'll see a lot of information on what a pressure cooker is, how it came to be, how to select one, how to use it, and some recipes to get you started. Take time to read the whole book, and get the most out of your cooker. In no time at all, you will become master of your own culinary destiny.

Bon apatite

Modern Day Pressure Cookers

Thankfully, the art of pressure cooking was evolved by the issuance of a U.S. Patent for an electric pressure-cooker, in 1991. Taking advantage of current technology, the new First Generation electric pressure cookers used electronic sensors to continuously monitor and control temperature and pressure. New safety features that would not allow the lid to be opened when the unit was under pressure were incorporated into the designs. The Second Generation of electric pressure-cookers came out in the mid-90s, and featured convenient functions such as digital presets, delayed cooking, automatic warm and hold functions, and a 'Leaky Lid" alarm that detects when the valve is open, or the seal is not working, and shuts itself off and sounds an alarm. The Third Generation of electric pressure cookers feature a microprocessor, which means each unit has a little computer but into it. Using highly sensitive digital sensors, these unit can perform all kinds of complicated

Third Generation 'Smart" Pressure-Cookers

cooking operations with the touch of a button. For example, many have setting for 'Multi-Grains', which means raw grain can be added to the cooker, and it will hold it for soaking at a specified temperature, before heating up to cooking temperatures.

They can be set for delayed cooking, and warming, which means that a person can load it, specify a time to start cooking, and then the unit will keep the food warm for up to two days, depending on the unit. So, you can load it in the morning, go to work and have dinner ready when you get home. The only thing it won't do it put it on the plate for you. Anyone can use these units. Cooking doesn't get any simpler than this.

All three types of electric pressure cookers are available, and what type you use just depends on how much hands-on control you want. Some of us prefer a little more, and some less. It's your choice. Many newer models, like the Wolfgang Puck Bistro Elite, have some features of all three types. The quality of these pressure cookers varies by manufactures, and runs the complete range from semi-professional quality, to cheap junk. Many will tell you to avoid electric pressure cookers because they are unreliable and are plagued with problems (before writing this book, I myself was one of these detractors...), but this is just because the market is still flooded with very cheap, poorly-made products. You're better off sticking to proven brands such as Presto, Cuisinart, Fagor, Emeril, Wolfgang Puck, Instant Pot, Nesco, etc. Avoid off- brand, or discount units. A high-quality modern electric pressure cooker is an outstanding appliance, safe, reliable, and a very good addition to any kitchen.

How It Works-The Secret Behind the Magic Trick

To understand how a pressure cooker works, you'll need to know just a teeny bit about physics. Don't get nervous. I won't be discussing Einstein's Unified Field Theory, Quantum Mechanics, or anything like that. Just plain gas physics, and not much of that.

We need only be concerned with a few fundamental physical laws, the main one being the Ideal Gas Law. Without all the scary mathematics, it just says that water under pressure can reach a higher temperature than the normal boiling point of 212°F. It is derived from Boyle's Law, Charles' Law, Avogadro's Law, and Amonton's Law. Sounds kind of like a physicists poker game, doesn't it? All these laws mean, as far as the home cook is concerned, is that under normal circumstances, water boils at 212°F. Once that temperature is reached the water will get no hotter, nor will the steam, no matter how much heat is applied. The Ideal Gas Law adds a closed-system to the deal, where pressure from the steam can build up. What this means for you is that now, the water and steam can reach considerably greater temperatures than 212°F. At 15 psi (normal cooking pressure), the temperature inside your pressure cooker is actually around 275°F.

This is exactly what a pressure cooker does. Other parts of these laws deal with heat transfer. Under pressure, steam has 6 times the heat potential, meaning it is 6 times more efficient at transferring its heat energy to a cooler object. To illustrate this, if you briefly put your hand in a 350°F oven, you won't get burned immediately. If you leave you hand in there, in a moment or so, the heat will get uncomfortable, and in a few minutes, it will start to hurt, and you will remove it, but no tissue has actually been damaged at this point. However, if you put your hand over the spout of a boiling tea kettle at 212°F, even for an instant, you hand will immediate be scalded, and blisters will soon appear. Your tissue has been damaged by the brief contact. That's because the steam transfers heat much faster than air. Under pressure, it is even 6 times more efficient. So now you have an idea of how a pressure cooker works.

There is one other factor worth mentioning. In conventional cooking methods, the outside of the food gets hot, and the heat is slowly transferred to the inside, meaning the outside of your food is well-done, and the inside barely cooked. Under pressure, the food is at the same temperature inside and out, whether it is one chicken leg, or a 15 lb. turkey. So the food is cooked evenly, inside and out. Isn't physics wonderful? Now that we know the theory, we can get into the nuts and bolts.

Here is a typical pressure cooker:

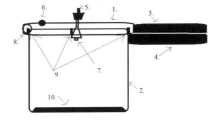

1. Lid - this goes on top (self-explanatory)

2. Pot - this holds the food, water and pressure

3. Lid Handle - this is so you can remove the lid without burning your hand. On a pressure cooker, the lid, and pot handles are designed

so that you can use both at once, to move the entire unit from the stove, or off a burner when needed. Electric cookers do not need these.

4. Pot Handle - so you can move the pot, when needed.

5. Pressure Regulator - this is just a weight, with a cone-shaped bottom. The weight is just heavy enough so that when the proper pressure is reached, steam pressure can come up through the vent and move it to the side, allowing a 'poof' of steam to come out, and keep the internal pressure constant. The weight moving from side-to-side is what gives pressure cookers their characteristic sss-sss-sss-sss sound when cooking. Since electric pressure cookers have sensors that regulate the temperature and pressure, this part is redundant, but still included as an extra safety feature. This is why electric cookers are so much quieter. The regulator is seldom 'tripped'.

6. Over-Pressure Plug - a rubber plug that pops out when the internal pressure reaches dangerous levels. It immediately reduces pressure. This is not required on electric cookers because they have automatic emergency shut-off circuitry.

7. Vent Pipe - allows steam to escape when needed to regulate pressure.

8. Sealing Gasket - makes an airtight seal between the pot and lid.

9. Friction Lid Locks - holds the lid on when the unit is under pressure.

10. Food Rack - keeps food off of the bottom of the pot, and out of direct contact with the liquid.

Pretty simple, huh? Not bad for a gadget that was invented in the 1600s. This is just a bare-bones basic cooker. They come a lot fancier, with pressure indicators, and such, but they all do the same thing. Electric pressure cookers are the same as well...almost. Because of modern technology, electric cookers are much 'smarter' and safer. They have sensors that tell the main control circuitry what is happening inside the cooker at all times. Then the controls make whatever adjustments are necessary, including a complete shut-down, if needed. And if any of the sensors fail, it shuts itself off. That's why you can just load them, set the time, and forget about it until the time is up.

Electric cookers have other neat features as well. One of the biggest dangers of the old stove-top pressure cookers was opening the lid before all the pressure was gone, meaning you had to scrape your supper from the ceiling and walls, and tend to semi-serious 2nd degree burns as well. This was probably the very first recipe ever done in a pressure cooker back in the 1600s....Projectile Chicken. Modern electric pressure cookers are designed so that it is difficult, if not impossible to open the lid if there is any remaining pressure inside. Most models are programmable, so that you can load them, set the timer, and they will start cooking at that time, then hold the food at a warm temperature, some models for up to 2 days. So you could load the unit, and have supper ready for you when you come home from work. Aaaaaah! Modern technology.... got to love it...

So, here is what happens when you cook in a modern electric pressure cooker. Add some water-based liquid (never use any oils by themselves. We'll discuss that in the safety section....) to the bottom, add your food, and put on the lid. After you seal the lid, and close the vent, both the temperature and pressure rise until the inside is at 15 psi, and roughly 275°F., if you remembered to turn the unit on...(don't laugh... it's happened to the best of us). Sensors constantly monitor both pressure, and temperature, and send signals to the heating elements, causing them to make whatever adjustments are needed to maintain this environment. If there is any deviation whatsoever from this environment, the sensors immediately send an emergency signal to the heating elements to shut down, NOW! This happens long before there is any danger of damage to your unit. It also happens if pressure does not stay at the proper levels. Some models even have an audible (meaning "loud and irritating") alarm that will go off when this happens. Digital models will display an error message informing you of what it thinks is wrong. The usual cause of this situation is simply the gasket not being seated properly, or being too worn out to create a seal.

If none of the above happens, your cooker is happily steaming away at 15 psi, and 275°F. Your food reaches cooking temperatures, both inside and outside, at the same rate as the steam, so cooking is immediate. Since there is more pressure outside of the food, than inside (more of those physics laws...), moisture, nutrients, and flavor is being driven into the food, rather than leaching out, as in conventional cooking methods. That's why it takes much less spice, and the food tastes sooooo much better in a pressure cooker. Since, according to those laws we talked about earlier, the steam is now super-efficient about transferring heat, the food cooks in a fraction of the time, even if frozen.

And that's how your pressure cooker works. Modern electric pressure cookers are so easy and safe to use that you may find yourself seldom using other methods. You may also find that you are eating less, because the food retains more of its nutrition, and is more filling and satisfying.

A good electric pressure cooker could be the perfect solution for creating healthy meals, while still maintaining a busy schedule. More and more people are turning to pressure cooking with electric cookers as a way to eat healthier, and still be productive. In today's fast-paced world of 'grab what you can, when you can' eating habits, with the attendant food additives, excess fats, salt, msg, and other not-so-desirable tidbits in 'fast', and processed foods, an electric pressure cooker may be just what you need.

Perfect....Anything

It's so easy to cook in these pressure cookers that instead of giving you an individual recipe for each thing, I can just tell you the technique, and you can create your own culinary masterpieces.

You can cook any meat or vegetables in your cooker. This recipe will work for pork, turkey, lamb, chicken, beef, or game meats. Just consult the Cooking Time Chart to set the timer. If you want to mix things, try to use meats that have similar cooking times if possible. Otherwise, use the cooking time for the longest cooking ingredient. For game meats, use the closest thing on the timer, ie; Beef for deer, elk, moose, antelope, etc... Chicken for squirrel, rabbit, opossum, doves, quail, etc...

This recipe also works with fish, but you need to wrap the fish in parchment paper so that it won't fall apart. Carp is especially delicious prepared like this. Just season each piece like you want, and add a veggie or two, or a slice of lemon, or lime, if desired, wrap the pieces individually and stack them on the rack, which you set on the vegetables, or other ingredients. When you open the packets (I just slit the paper across the top and serve it in the packet, to hold in the juices), you will be amazed at the tender, moist fish, just full of flavor!

- Large pieces of meat, or any roast that will fit in the cooker.
- Your favorite vegetables (potatoes, broccoli, carrots, celery, etc...)
- Salt, pepper, spices to taste.
- 2 cups of water
- Add water to the cooker.
- Add vegetables to the bottom.
- Rub meat with your favorite spices.

Place rack on top of veggies (you can omit this step, It really doesn't matter much. It just makes it a little easier to remove the meat after cooking), or set the meat directly on top of veggies.

Set the timer for whatever meat you are cooking. If you are not sure, beef and pork will absolutely cook all the way in 45 minutes to an hour (45 for thawed, 1 hour for frozen), usually a lot less. But 45 minutes will almost always work. Chicken goes about 10-20 minutes, maybe 30 if frozen solid. Turkey roast, about 1 hour, or 90 minutes if frozen. Fish, 5 minutes, or 10 if frozen. You really don't have to worry much about over-cooking in these cookers. They are very forgiving.

When the time is up, either let the pressure reduce on its own, or vent it manually.

Remove the lid, place food on plates, and chow down and remember to save the liquid to use in other recipes. That's really all there is to it.

I also want to add some information on using the recipes in this book using the Instant Pot. The Instant Pot has become the best selling pressure cooker in North America.

Using the Instant Pot with the recipes in this book.

The recipes in this book were designed and tested with a Wolfgang Puck Bistro 6 Qt. pressure cooker. It is very simple with only a few button. "Cook", "Warm" and "Heat" and a timer. It is pre-set for Cooking at high pressure. The newer more advanced electric pressure cookers come with many different functions and pre-set buttons. The Instant Pot Electric Pressure Cooker has now become the best selling pressure cooker in North America.

If you have an Instant Pot, you can use these recipes with just a few adjustments.

The Instant Pot has 14 function keys, 9 used for cooking different food.

Soup, Meat/Stew, Bean/Chili, Poultry, Rice, Multigrain, Porridge, Steam and Manual.

Each one of these have pre-set cooking times and some can be adjusted. You can learn more about this in the Instant Pot instruction manual and videos that they have on- line.

To use these recipes with the Instant Pot I suggest just using two of the buttons. The "Sauté" button and The "Manual" button. The manual button is an all-purpose button that is pre-set at high pressure (You can also adjust it to low pressure buy pushing the pressure button) Mostly all the recipes in this book are for high pressure.

The cooking time can be adjusted with the + and – keys. It can perform as any of the pre-set keys do.

I use the manual button mostly when I use my instant pot.

You will notice that when a recipe in this book calls for browning it usually says "heat the oil in the pressure cooker

Pressure cooker in the "heat" or "sauté" mode. With the Instant Pot just press the sauté button and wait for the display to read "Hot" before adding the oil, butter or any food. Since the inner pot is stainless steel, this is the preferred method. After following the recipe instructions and the sautéing is done, press cancel.

This will turn off the sauté mode and the cooker will be ready for the next step. Add the remaining ingredients as per the recipe. Cover and lock the lid and set the pressure valve to "sealing".

Press the manual button and set the timer according to the recipe.

When the pressure cooking cycle is done the beeper sounds, release the pressure If the recipe calls for a manual or quick release, turn the pressure valve to the "venting" position.

When the pressure is fully released the float valve will drop and the cover will become unlocked

If the recipe calls for a natural release, turn off or unplug the cooker and wait till the pressure releases.

When the pressure is fully released the float valve will drop and the cover will automatically unlock.

Just to recap…

Press the sauté button, when the display reads "Hot" and the oil or butter. When the oil or butter is hot add the ingredients that need to be browned or sautéed. When this step is done press the cancel button.

Continue on with the recipe instructions and when it is time to set the pressure, press the manual button and adjust the time according to the recipe. Close and lock the lid and seal the pressure valve. When the cooking time is up and the beeper sounds release the pressure as per the recipe instructions.

That's really all there is to it.

Tips, Tricks and Techniques

Pressure cooking is easy, but there are a lot of tricks you can use to make your food even better. None of them are very difficult, and they can really enhance both the flavor, and appearance of your culinary creations.

- **Basic Cooking:** It is really hard to mess up with a modern pressure cooker, especially the electric ones. One time, I put the lid on without checking the seal, and it never developed pressure, but the chicken and corn on the cob I had in it still came out delicious. I don't recommend this, but this is just to calm any fears you might have about using pressure cookers. Most have safety devices to keep you from doing anything too dangerous, like opening the lid when there is pressure in the unit. And you really don't even need a recipe for most things. Since a lot of spice is not needed, in some cases, none at all, you can just throw stuff in the cooker, add liquid (at least 1 cup), lock the lid, close the vent, set the timer, and let it do it's thing. If you miscalculated on the time, and your food is under-done, just put the lid back on, and add more time on the timer. If you cook it too long, the worst thing that will usually happen is that your food will be super-tender (even seafood, which usually gets tough when over-cooked in a conventional oven...). If you added enough water, it is difficult to burn your food, unless you go out for a few hours and leave it cooking with little water in it. Since it is a closed system, the water cannot evaporate out. You only lose a small fraction through the vent. Most of the water keeps circulating as steam.

One of the most basic tips is that when you are using raw onions, garlic and other quick-cooking ingredients, the flavor can be concentrated by sautéing them first. Heat up your cooker, and add some oil, or better yet, fry a piece of bacon, fat-back or salt pork in the pot. You can also add wine, beer, liquor, tea or anything else you want to flavor it with. When the onions get translucent, add the liquid, and proceed with your recipe.

Sometimes, you may want a little bit of a crust on your meat. Warm up the cooker and add a little oil to the bottom. Now, add your meat, and brown it on all sides. Just add liquid when you are ready to stop the browning process. Or, you can transfer things like pasta and marinara sauce into a casserole dish, top with mozzarella cheese, and place it in a hot oven until the cheese melts and gets a little brown, for a fantastic Italian casserole.

White rice takes on a whole new flavor when it is toasted before cooking. Add some oil, or butter, to the bottom of the warm pot, add your rice, and stir it occasionally, until it gets a nice light tan color. Add liquid to stop the browning process. Now, just add water or stock, and set the timer to the correct time for the type of rice you are cooking.

Another wonderful thing about pressure cookers is that you don't have to pre-soak beans and grains. You can make delicious beans by just putting them in the cooker with the required amount of water (some beans need more water than others. Check the chart for liquid and cooking times) , a little salt and pepper to taste, and setting the timer for the correct time for the type of beans. They will come out fully cooked, and creamy, with plenty of natural flavor. Whole grains become a culinary treat when served as side dishes, or even main servings for hot breakfast cereals. Bulgar wheat, whole wheat berries, barley, amaranth, millet and other grains can be cooked and eaten just like rice, and oat groats can be flaked, steel-cut with a hand-grinder, or cooked whole for a delicious breakfast repast.

If you want to cook with things that may foam, just add a tbsp. of oil. This will prevent foaming.

Unless you are making pudding, most of the time, you don't want milk to boil or scald. When making cream soups and sauces, add your milk after the main ingredients have cooked, and let it finish with the lid off. This also works for cheese sauces as well.

If you want a crust on your entrée, like ribs, chicken, etc...., after pressure cooking, you can transfer the food to the oven and bake for 10-15 minutes to create a nice, crispy crust.

Special Techniques

You may not realize it, but your pressure cooker can do many other things besides pressure cook. Try these techniques out and you'll see how a pressure cooker, especially the electric ones, can be one of the most versatile appliances in your kitchen.

- **Popcorn:** You won't believe how perfect your pressure cooker can make popcorn, where almost every kernel pops, and not a single one scorched. It takes about 3 minutes to pop 1/3 cup of popcorn.

Step 1: Heat up the cooker, set the timer for 30 minutes (time doesn't really matter...it's just to heat up the cooker...omit the timer with a stove-top cooker) and add a little oil to the bottom, just enough to cover it (in this case I am using olive oil because...well, I just like olive oil).

Step 2: Allow the oil to heat for a few minutes.

Step 3: Add the popcorn and put on the lid, but don't lock it, and don't close the vent.

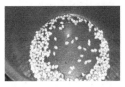

Step 4: You will hear the popcorn when it starts to pop. It may take a few minutes, but it will start. When the popping slows down, turn the timer to '0', or remove the cooker from the heat source. Do not open the lid, yet.

Step 5: When it sounds like all the popping is done (there is always one kernel that will wait until the lid is off to pop, no matter how long you leave it...), remove the lid and transfer the corn to a serving bowl. Add salt, butter, or whatever you want, and enjoy!

Your pressure cooker is also great for making perfect boiled eggs:

Put enough cold water to cover the eggs in the pot. Leave the vent open. Add the eggs to the cold water.

Set the timer for 9 minutes for hard-boiled, 6 minutes for medium, and 3 for soft-boiled eggs. I set these for 9 minutes, to make egg salad with. As you can see, the eggs came out perfect, with nice creamy yolks that are not over-cooked and dry.

Another useful thing your pressure cooker can do is sterilize things. Glass jars, tweezers, scissors, and other things can be made 100% sterile by placing them on the trivet, locking the lid, closing the vent, and setting the timer for 5 minutes or so. Just be careful not to put anything in it that might melt, like things with plastic handles. And be careful with metal items, so you don't scratch the non-stick surface inside the pot.

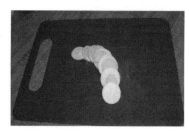

You can also use your pressure cooker for hot towels. Just fold a towel (one that will fit) and place it on the trivet, and pour a cup of water in the bottom of the pot. Lock the lid, close the vent and set the timer for 3 minutes. You'll probably have to let the towel cool a little before you can handle it, but it makes a nice hot towel for shaving.

■ Using Inserts: Most pressure cookers come with a rack, called a trivet that keeps food from direct contact with the bottom of the pan, where the heat originates. This is to prevent scorching, but it is also handy for cooking two things at once. For example, you can layer the bottom with corn on the cob, or whole potatoes, add the water, then put the rack on top of the veggies. Now, place a whole chicken, roast, pork loin, pork chops, en papilotte packs (more on this coming up...), or anything else you want on top of the rack, lock the lid, close the vent, and let 'er go. The flavors of the different ingredients blend, meld, enhance each other, and do all kinds of wonderful things when left on their own. Try to select things that all have similar cooking times. As long as everything will cook within 5 -7 minutes of each other, you're good to go. Be creative.... If your trivet doesn't have handles to make it easy to remove it, you can make a pair from folded up foil. This makes it easy to remove things like a whole chicken, which may fall apart if you try to lever it out with spatulas.....

There are several ways to cook in a pressure cooker. The easiest is just to throw everything in, add water and set the timer. I have included some "dump" recipes later in the recipe section. This is fine for things that have similar cooking times, but what if you want to cook things with greatly different cooking times, such as a beef stew with brisket. Brisket takes a little while to tenderize, and your potatoes and carrots would undoubtedly turn to mush. To get around this problem, use the phased cooking method. Just put your brisket in the cooker with enough water, and cook it until it is done. Then, just do a manual pressure release (or use the cold water method with a stop-top cooker), add the potatoes, carrots and other stuff, put on the lid, close the vent and continue cooking until the veggies are done. For cooking several things at once, but still keep them separate, you can use the tiered cooking method. All you do is put the different items in separate pans that will fit in the cooker, and layer them (but not more than 3/4 of the way full), one on top of another. Some models come with stackable pans, and after-market kits are easily available. You may come across some cookers that call themselves infusion cookers. Don't be miss-lead. It is just a marketing ploy to get you to buy another expensive kitchen appliance. All pressure cookers are infusion cookers. That's the way they work. They drive the flavor of your cooking water, and the foods own natural juices deep into the food, instead of leaching it out. That's why you don't need a lot of spices. Want some smoked chicken, but only have a hour or so to cook? Put 2 cups of water in your cooker, along with 6 or 7 drops of Liquid Smoke, and maybe a little garlic powder. Add a whole chicken (on the trivet, so you can get it back out in one piece), close the lid, seal the vent and cook for 20 minutes or so. Ease the bird out, and.... instant smoked chicken. It tastes just like it's been in the smoker for 6 or 7 hours, except is isn't nearly as dry. Next time, try using orange juice instead of water. Add barbecue sauce to the liquid. Cook your rice in Green Tea. Try doing a ham in Coca Cola, Pepsi, or (delicious) 7-Up. Add some maple syrup to the liquid the next time you do a chicken or ham. Go ahead...be creative.

There is no hard and fast formula for converting a regular recipe to a pressure cooker one. But the good news is that pressure cookers are incredibly forgiving. A few basic guidelines are to limit the amount of fats and oils to no more than 1/4 cup, total. Add milk and dairy products after pressure cooking, so they won't scorch. Reduce liquids by at least 1/3, because the water will not evaporate in a pressure cooker. It is a closed system. Except for what the food absorbs, what you put in is what you will get out. Reduce the cooking times by 2/3rds, and be sure to use the cooking time charts if you are not sure. Add thickening agents such as roux, flour, cornstarch, etc...After pressure cooking. Just allow the food to continue cooking with the lid off until the desired thickness is achieved.

To troubleshoot, there really isn't much to worry about. Only a few things can happen, and none are really that bad. If you used too much water (not really a bad thing), you can ladle the extra liquid out, and save it to use in future recipes. It will freeze just fine. If you didn't use enough liquid, your first warning will be a scorched smell. Immediately reduce pressure manually, and check the food. It will probably be just a little scorched on the bottom, and the rest will be salvageable. Just trim the crispy stuff off, and save it to use in other recipes, or give it to the dog, cat, garbage disposal, or whatever, and pay more attention next time. If you really over-cooked the veggies, to where they are just mush, remove the meat, and use an immersion blender or pour it into a regular blender, and puree it all into a rich gravy. Serve it over the meat. No one will be the wiser. If you didn't cook the food long enough, just put the lid back on, seal the vent and cook it a little longer. That's really all there is to it.

One final tip: When you are carrying the pressure cooker, be sure to use the side carry handles, and not the lid handle (that's how I broke mine.....).

Bon apetit

Maintenance and Repair

If something breaks or goes wrong with your cooker, repair and service depends on the brand. Stove-top models like Presto are easy to find replacement parts for, and most major brands have outstanding Customer Service. Electric models are a little more difficult to get parts and service for. Most of these are not manufactured by the company that is selling them. The vast majority are manufactured in China, and replacement parts are difficult to find. Customer Service on most of these is non-existent. A case in point. The handle on my Electric Wolfgang Puck Bistro Elite broke where the screws go in to hold it to the lid. Numerous calls to their 'Customer Service' number were answered by a machine telling me to leave my number, and no option for getting anyone with a pulse on the line. All of my calls went unanswered. The only call that was answered by a real human-being was to the Sales Department, who transferred me to the 'Customer Service' department as soon as they realized that I did not want to buy anything. They were unimpressed that my unit should have still been under warranty. I was able to find some replacement parts at http://www.wpcookware. com/categories.asp?cat=29, but they only had the complete lid assembly, for $53.00. I wound up repairing the handle myself with a $3.00 tube of 5-minute epoxy from Ace Hardware.

Not pretty, but it works......

For $53.00, I could probably have a Fabrication Shop make me a complete new handle out of wood, or aluminum that would never break again. I will probably be doing that soon. This cooker was only 3 months old when the handle broke.

On the good side, the website does have the most important replacement part you will need...the gasket. More on that later.

No matter how good a unit is made, it will not last long if it is not taken care of. And the very first thing to do to make sure your unit lasts, is to disassemble it, and clean every part of it after each use. Pay special attention to the gasket, and the vent. Make sure the vent is clean and free by running water through it. The gasket should be oiled with vegetable oil every few months to keep it from drying out.

Cleaning a stove-top pressure cooker is easy, but electric ones are a bit tricker, because they cannot be submerged, and you have to be careful not to get water in the digital circuits, or it will ruin the readouts and sensors. Here are the steps to clean an electric cooker:

■ Clean the outside- remove the electric cord and the inner cooking pot. Wipe the outside of the unit with a clean, damp (not wet) cloth. Stubborn spots can be removed by wetting them with vinegar, and letting it set for 5 minutes, then wipe it off. The inside can be wiped with a very damp cloth, and allowed to air dry. Wipe off the cord with a damp cloth. A toothbrush, or similar brush can be used to clean out the plug receptacle. You can use electrical contact cleaners like Blow Off, but be sure to dry the contacts well, before using the unit again.

■ Clean the inner pot-this can be cleaned just like any other pot, taking care not to use anything abrasive that might damage the non-stick surface. Do not use steel wool, Scotchbrite, greenies, SOS pads, or similar pads, but the plastic scouring pads are OK. Make sure the outside is dry before using it again.

■ Cleaning the lid-this is one of the most critical parts. Remove the Pressure Valve and rinse it well with hot water. Remove the gasket, and sealing ring, and rinse them well. Coat them with a little vegetable oil. Remove the Anti-Block cover, and rinse it well. Rinse the lid with hot water (detergent is usually not necessary), and wipe the inner surface of the lid with a damp cloth, paying special attention to the gasket channel, the areas around the float-valve, pressure limit valve, air escape valve, and the anti-block cover. Make sure water flows freely through the Pressure Valve, and Float Valves. Remember to put all the parts back in the lid before using the unit again.

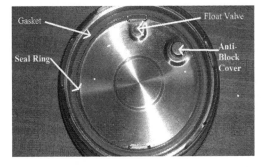

Everything should be dried before using the unit.

Here are a few maintenance tips that will greatly increase the life-span of your cooker.

■ Clean the unit after every use.

■ Replace damaged gaskets, and seal rings. Anytime there are cracks, they need need replaced. It's a good idea to always have a spare gasket, and seal ring. Be sure to coat the new ones with vegetable oil before installing.

■ Store the unit with the lid on top, upside-down, with the weight setting in the middle. This allows air to circulate inside and retard the growth of mold and bacteria.

■ If you won't be using the unit for a few weeks, store the gasket and seal ring in a Zip-Lok baggie with with a little dry baking soda. Store the bag in the unit. Also, add a teaspoon or so of baking soda to the bottom of the inner cooking pot. This removes odors, and moisture build-up.

■ It is possible to restore a gasket and seal ring that has just started to crack, by coating it with vegetable oil, but I do not recommend it. Gaskets and seal rings are cheap, and it's not worth taking the chance of a catastrophic failure. The rings are one of the most critical parts of the entire unit.

■ Never overfill the cooker. 3/4 full is plenty, to allow for expansion of the food during cooking. Over-filling can block the valves, resulting in damage to the unit, and a possible dangerous situation.

■ Make sure there is at least 1/2 cup of water in the cooking pot before pressure-cooking. Allowing the cooker to run dry can damage the seals and gaskets.

■ Never use chlorine bleach to clean the unit. Chlorine can react with the metal in the cooker.

■ Never leave a stove-top pressure cooker unattended when being used. They lack the automatic safety features of electric cookers. Electric cookers can be safely left alone while cooking.

■ With just a little care, your pressure cooker can last a lifetime, or longer.

PART TWO

· ·

Appendix A

Cooking Times

Beans and Legumes Cooking Times

There are hundreds of varieties of edible beans and legumes. If you want to cook one that is not listed here, just use the cooking times for the closest one.

For most beans, it is not necessary to measure out the liquid. You can just covert them with liquid to a depth of 1" to 2". Too much liquid will not hurt your beans. You can simply take them out with a slotted spoon. If you are guessing, it's better to have too much water, rather than not enough. Besides, soupy beans are great with cornbread......

Bean/Legume	Cooking Time (unsoaked)	Liquid-2:1 unless the recipe says otherwise
Adzuki	25	
Anasazi	45	
Beans, black	35	
Beans, garbanzo (chickpeas)	45	3 to 1
Beans, great northern	30	3 to 1
Beans, lima, baby	30	
Beans, lima, large	35	
Beans, navy or pea or white (haricot)	60	3 to 1
Beans, pinto	30	3 to 1
Beans, red kidney	30	4 to 1
Beans, soy (beige)	35	
Beans, soy (black)	35	
Beans, white kidney (cannellini)	45	4 to 1
Cranberry (romano or borlotti)	60	
Gandules	45	
Lentils, green, mini (brown)	15	
Lentils, red, split	15	
Lentils, yellow, split (moong dal)	15	
Peas, split, green or yellow	15	
Peas, dried, whole	15	
Peas, black eyed	30	
Scarlet runner	30	

Grains and Rice

Always use the natural release method to reduce pressure when cooking grains. Always add a little oil to prevent foaming.

Grains	Ratio-Grain to Water	Cooking Time (minutes)
Barley, pearl	1:4	15 to 20
Barley, pot	1:3	20
Bulgur	1:3	8 to 10
Couscous	1:2	2 to 3
Kamut, whole	1:3	10 to 12
Oats, quick cooking	1:1-1/3	6
Oats, steel-cut	1:1-2/3	11
Quinoa, quick cooking	1:2	6
Rice, basmati	1:1-1/2	5 to 7
Rice, brown	1:1-1/2	12 to 15
Rice, white	1:1-1/2	5 to 6
Rice, wild	1:3	22 to 25
Spelt berries	1:3	15
Wheat berries	1:3	30

Meat and Poultry Cooking Times

These cooking times are approximate. Many things can affect the cooking time, such as altitude, humidity, the type and model of your cooker, etc...You may have to adjust your cooking time slightly.

It would be impossible to list all the animals that could be eaten. For anything not listed, use the cooking time for the next closest thing., such as chicken cooking times for rattlesnake and frog legs, pork for animals with a high fat content, like opossum and beaver, etc...

Item	Cooking Time (add 30% if frozen)	Liquid
Beef, 1" cubes, 1-1/2 lb	10 to 15	At least 1 cup, unless the recipe says otherwise.
Beef, brisket, thawed, 4-5 lbs	80 minutes	" "
Beef, heart, 3 to 4 lb	50 to 75	" "
Beef, kidneys	8 to 10	" "
Beef, liver	5	" "
Beef, meatballs, 1 to 2 lb	4 to 9	" "
Beef, meatloaf, 2 lb	10 to 15	" "
Beef, oxtail	40 to 45	" "
Beef, pot roast, rump, round, chuck, blade or brisket, 1-1/2 lb to 2 lb	35 to 40	" "
Beef, ribs, short, grilling	25	" "
Beef, ribs, short, stewing	35	" "
Beef, shanks, 1-1/2" wide	25 to 30	" "
Beef, steak, rump, round, chuck or blade, 1 to 2"	20 to 25	" "
Beef, stew meat, 1-1/2" cubes	15	" "
Goat, 3 lb	25	" "
Elk, Deer, Moose, Antelope, Caribou, 2-3 lb	25-30	" "

Item	Cooking Time (add 30% if frozen)	Liquid
Game Birds (dove, quail, pigeon, starling, partridge, etc..)	8-12	" "
Chicken, breasts, boneless, skinless fillets, 2 to 3 lb	10-15	" "
Chicken, drumsticks (legs) or thighs	10-15	" "
Chicken, ground	4, thawed 7 frozen	" "
Chicken, liver	3, thawed 5 frozen	" "
Chicken, strips, boneless	6-10	" "
Chicken, whole, 2 to 3 lb	18 to 25	" "
Chicken, whole, 3 to 4 lb	25 to 30	" "
Ostrich, 2-3 lb	10/12/12	" "
Cornish Hen, whole	8 to 10	" "
Pheasant, whole	15-20	
Duck, pieces	8 to 10	" "
Duck, whole 3 to 4 lb	25 to 30	" "
Lamb, 1" cubes, 1 1/2 lb	10 to 18	" "
Lamb, chops, 1" thick	10	" "
Lamb, leg	35 to 40	" "
Lamb, stew meat	12 to 15	" "
Pork, ham shank, 2 lb	20 to 25	" "
Pork, ham, pieces	20 to 25	" "
Pork, hocks, smoked (cover completely w/ liquid)	40 to 50	" "
Pork, ribs, 2 lb	15	" "
Pork, 3 lb roast	30 to 45	" "
Turkey, breast, boneless	20	" "
Turkey, breast, whole, with bone in	20 to 30	" "
Turkey, drumsticks (leg)	12	" "
Bear, Beaver and Nutria, 3-4 lb roast	35-40	" "
Small Game (opossum, squirrel, woodchuck, rabbit) 2 lb	12/14/12	" "

Seafood and Fish Cooking Times

Seafood and fish are delicious in a pressure cooker, when done properly. Remember, most fish will be very delicate, so they are best cooked en papillote. Bivalve mollusks, such as clams, and mussels, that are normally cooked in the shell, should be cooked until the shells pop open. They tend to be on the tough side, so longer cooking times are better than less. Squid and Octopus need to be cooked for long times to break-down the rubbery texture.

* Do not put live crabs, lobsters, octopus or squid in your pressure cooker. In the first place, it is inhumane, because they will be suffering while the heat and pressure builds up inside, and second, they can damage the inside of your cooker, and/or block the vent while trying to escape. Kill them humanely before cooking.

Item	Cooking Times (add 20% if frozen)	Liquid
Crabs, up to 3 lbs	3 to 6	At least 1 cup, unless the recipes specifies otherwise.
Eel	9	" "
Fish fillets 2-3 lbs	6-8	" "
Fish steak 2-3 lbs	10-15	" "
Fish, whole dressed 2-3 lbs	12-15	" "
Fish soup or stock, 2 quarts	12-15	" "
Shark, Tuna, Swordfish, 2 lbs	7	
Lobster and Langostino, 1 1/2 to 2 lbs	2 to 3	" "
Mussels and Clams, in the shell	7 to 10	" "
Shrimp, Prawns and Crayfish	3 to 6	" "
Oysters, shelled, any amount	3 to 6	" "
Scallops, any amount	3 to 6	" "
Abalone, any amount	3 to 6	" "
Squid, 2-3 lbs	30-40	" "
Octopus, 2-3 lbs	40-45	" "
Paella Mix, 2 lbs	15	" "

Vegetable Cooking Times

It would be impossible to list all edible vegetables available world-wide here. For a veggie not listed, just use the time for the closest thing, such as potato cooking times for yami, or greens for dandelion, etc... Vegetables with similar textures have similar cooking times. Most veggies require minimum cooking.

Vegetable	Cooking Time (add 20% if frozen)	Liquid-at least 1cup, unless the recipe says otherwise
Artichoke, large whole,	9 to 12	
Artichoke, medium whole,	6 to 9	
Artichoke, small whole,	3 to 6	
Artichoke, hearts	3	
Asparagus spears	3	
Green Beans	3	
Beets, 1/4" slices	6	
Beet greens	3	
Yellow, or Wax Beans	3	
Broccoli, flowerets	3	
Broccoli, stalks	6	
Broccoli, stalks, 1/4" slices	3 to 5	
Brussel Sprouts	4	
Cabbage	3 to 5	
Cactus (Nopales), whole paddles	12	
Cactus (Nopales) sliced	9	
Carrots, 1/4" slices	3	
Carrots, 1" slices	5	
Cattails	8	

Vegetable	Cooking Time (add 20% if frozen)	Liquid-at least 1cup, unless the recipe says otherwise
Cauliflower	3	
Celery,	3	
Greens (turnip, mustard, collard, etc...)	5	
Corn, kernels	1	
Corn on the cob	3	
Corn, dried (also dried Hominy)	30 to 45	
Day Lilies	3	
Dandelion	3	
Eggplant	3	
Endive,	3	
Escarole	3	
Kale	3	
Kudzu	3	
Leeks	3 to 5	
Mixed vegetables, frozen	3	
Okra	6	
Onions	3	
Parsnips	3	
Snow Peas	3	
English Peas	3	
Split Peas, dried	15	
Peppers (Jalapeño, Green, Chile, etc..)	6	
Polk Salad	12	
Potatoes, cubed	6 to 9	
Potatoes, new, whole small	9	
Potatoes, whole large	12 to 15	
Pumpkin	3	
Beets, fresh sliced	4	
Red beet, fresh whole	15	

Vegetable	Cooking Time (add 20% if frozen)	Liquid-at least 1cup, unless the recipe says otherwise
Rutabaga	6	
Spinach, fresh	3	
Spinach, frozen	6	
Squash, whole or halved	7	
Squash, sliced	3	
Sweet potato, cubed	6	
Sweet Potato, whole	12	
Swede	6	
Swiss chard	3	
Tomatoes, in quarters	3	
Tomatoes, whole	3	
Turnip, whole	9	
Turnip, sliced or cubed	3	
Zuchini, sliced	3	
Yami, Taro, Poi, Dasheen	9	
Yucca, Manioc, Cassava	12	

PART THREE

Recipes

Introduction to Recipes

Here is a collection of the 29 original easy recipes (with over 200 more later on) to get you started. This is by no means an all-inclusive list of what you can cook in a pressure cooker. I have tried to select recipes that showcase a particular technique, or style of cooking. You can use these as a base to expand your own creations. I also purposely did not include any real fancy recipes, or anything that would be beyond the skills of an average home cook. No one wants to come home from work, and then try to cook soufflés for a family of 4. These recipes are just simple good food, for real people. For now, we'll leave the fancy stuff to the 4-star restaurants.

I did include just some desserts because most sweets that are possible to create with a pressure cooker have been listed in countless other books, and on the Internet. However, I did add some unique ones. Pie fillings are very easy to make, and most puddings fair out better on the stove top. One exception is cheese cake filling. Pressure cooking enhances the flavor of the filling significantly. There are literally hundreds of pressure cooker cheesecake recipes on the Internet. Pick one and have fun with it. While it is possible to bake in a pressure cooker (sort of), the humid environment of the cooker leaves the finished product something less than ideal on cakes, brownies and breads. This is one technique that the pressure cooker will never replace. Baked goods should be baked, in a good oven.

In the appendix, and in the chapter on Tips and Tricks, there is a lot of information to help you develop your own recipes, and adapt your existing ones. I hope you enjoy exploring the world of pressure cookers as much as I did writing about it.

Sincerely

Joel C. Brothers

PS. Thanks to the 1000's of people who have purchased this book since its initial publication and the 100's of comments and suggestions that we have received. This information has helped us to add an additional 150 recipes. Hope you enjoy and continue to leave your feedback. comments and suggestions!

29 ORIGINAL RECIPES

Barbecue Pork

There's nothing like the taste of properly-done barbecue. But it takes a few days of planning, and 12+ hours of smoking to get it right......Well, not anymore. Your pressure cooker will make succulent, mouth-watering barbecue in just 1 hour. The pressure and steam drive the Liquid Smoke flavor right into the meat. It is only distinguishable from the old-fashioned way of cooking in that it is absolutely not dry. Try this recipe, and you may not ever want to use your outside smoker again.

- 1 Pork Roast (5-8 pounds)
- 24 ounces of your favorite barbecue sauce
- 2 cups water
- 1 tsp. garlic powder
- 1 tsp. Hickory Liquid Smoke
- Salt and pepper to taste

Pour 2 cups water in your cooker. Add the Liquid Smoke to the water. Rub the roast with the garlic, salt and pepper and place it in the cooker (you can use the rack if you want, but it really doesn't matter).

Set the time for 60 minutes, lock the lid on, move the vent to 'Seal', and find something to do for a while.

When the timer is done, allow pressure to reduce naturally. When the pressure is gone, open the lid, and carefully remove the roast to a large mixing bowl. Shred the pork with two forks (or allow it to cool and do it with your clean hands if you have that much patience...). The pork will be so tender that it is often enough just to touch it with the forks, and it will fall apart on its own. Set aside.

Pour the water/juice out of the cooker, but reserve it. Return the pork to the cooker. Add barbecue sauce, and enough of the reserved juice to get the consistency you want. Leave the lid off and set the time for 10 minutes. Allow the pork to simmer a bit in the sauce. Serve on buns with lots of potato salad and coleslaw.

Black Bean Salad

An outstanding salad with the great taste of Cancún

- 4 cups water
- 2 pounds black beans
- 2 slices salt pork, or ham hock, diced fine
- 1-15 oz. can of corn
- 1 cup fresh cilantro, chopped
- 2 tbsp. chili powder
- 1 tbsp. cumin
- 1/4 onion, diced fine
- 2 cloves garlic, crushed
- 2 avocados, peeled, and cut into 1" pieces
- 4 large green onions, cut into 1/4" thick slices
- 4 large fresh tomatoes, cut into 1" chunks
- 8 jalapeño peppers, with seeds and veins removed, cut into 1/4" pieces
- 2 tbsp. lime juice
- 1 tbsp. Extra Virgin olive oil
- 1 tsp. sugar
- Salt and pepper to taste

Plug in pressure cooker and set to heat or saute.

Add salt pork to the pot and cook until it makes some oil.

Add the diced onions (not the green ones) and garlic. Sauté until the onions get translucent.

Add water, beans, chili powder, cumin, salt and pepper, place the lid on the cooker and lock it, seal the pressure valve and set the timer for 30 minutes.

While the beans are cooking, cut all the other vegetables, except the avocado, and add them to a large mixing bowl. Add the corn to the bowl. Chop the cilantro and add it to the mixing bowl.

When the light goes to 'WARM', allow the pressure to reduce on its own (naturally). Place a colander in the sink. When the pressure is gone, open the cooker. Using oven mitts, remove the inner pot, take it to the sink, and carefully pour the beans into the colander and allow to drain. Rinse them with cold water until they are very cool, and add to the mixing bowl.

Peel the avocado, and cut into 1" chunks. Add the avocado to the mixing bowl.

Add the sugar, olive oil and lime juice, salt and pepper, and toss gently until well mixed. Transfer the salad to a container with a lid, and chill for at least 4 hours before serving.

Black Bean Soup

- 6 cups water or stock
- 1 lb. black beans (soaked or not)
- 12 oz. Chorizo, unwrapped and crumbled
- 1 large onion, chopped
- 1 large poblano, or bell pepper, chopped
- 3 cloves garlic, peeled and chopped
- 1 tbsp. chili powder
- 1 tbsp. dried oregano
- 1 tbsp. cumin
- 1 tsp. coriander
- 1 splash of lime juice, or beer
- Salt and pepper to taste

You can soak the beans in a brine overnight to concentrate the flavor, but you don't have to. You can use un-soaked beans. Just rinse them good, and check for rocks and bad beans.

Plug in the cooker, and set the timer for 45 minutes.

Add oil to the cooker and allow to heat.

Sauté chorizo, onions, bell pepper and garlic in the oil until the onions are translucent.

Add beans, remaining ingredients, and water. Close and lock the lid, close the vent, and allow to cook for the set time.

When time is up, allow the pressure to reduce naturally.

When pressure is gone, remove lid, and using an immersion blender, or food processor, puree the soup until smooth.

Garnish with fresh cilantro, avocado, sour cream, and serve with lots of hot corn tortillas.

Chicken and Sausage Cajun Gumbo

The real deal. I've used frozen veggies in this recipe for convenience, but you can substitute fresh ones. There are few rules where gumbo is concerned, except for one....there are no tomatoes in real gumbo! If a restaurant tries to serve you gumbo with tomatoes, send it back and go somewhere else. New Orleans tourists, and Creoles may eat tomatoes in their gumbo, but that is an entirely different animal. Few things will make a Cajun angrier. Another thing - do not wimp out and use peanut butter-colored roux. They may serve that light-colored stuff in New Orleans, but real Cajun gumbo uses black, or at least coffee-colored roux. Keep it cooking until you get the right color. It will be worth the extra trouble.

- 4 cups water
- 2 lb. smoked sausage, sliced
- 2 lbs. chicken parts (legs, thighs...whatever)
- 1 package frozen gumbo vegetables
- 1 cup black, or dk brown roux
- 4 cloves garlic, minced
- 1 onion, diced
- 1 green pepper, diced
- 2 ribs celery, sliced

- 1 tbsp. oil or butter
- 1 tsp. Cayenne pepper
- 4-7 drops MciIlhenny's Tabasco Sauce (do not substitute, this is the only real tabasco sauce)
- Salt and pepper to taste
- Cooked white rice
- For the roux:
- 1/2 cup flour
- 1/4 cup oil

A word about roux: Making quick roux is the most dangerous thing you ever do in your kitchen. It is 500°F and sticks to everything it touches. Restaurants refer to it as Cajun Napalm. When making roux, put the cats and dogs outside, send the children out to play, and get rid of any and all distractions. Let the phone ring. If anyone comes to the door, they can wait... Have all your utensils, and ingredients, especially oven mitts, handy, as well as a box of baking soda, in case of a flame up. Do not use butter, or any oil with a low flash-point. Save your olive oil for fancier dishes. Regular vegetable oil is OK to use. Peanut or cottonseed oil is the best.

Before cooking the gumbo, fire up the cooker and put 4 cups water in the bottom. Add the chicken, close the lid, seal the vent and set the timer for 30 minutes. When the timer is done, release pressure manually, remove the chicken, and liquid from the pot, debone, and remove skin from the chicken. Pull the meat into chunky pieces. Set the liquid aside. Don't worry about cleaning the pot. Just leave it on. You want the chicken residue in it.

Once you are done with the chicken, set the cooker to heat or sauté, add the oil to the pot and sauté the onions, garlic, peppers and celery until the onions are translucent.

Return the liquid you cooked the chicken in to the pot. Add the chicken, sausage, vegetables, Cayenne, Tabasco, salt and pepper. Allow to simmer while you are making the roux.

On the stove top, in a heavy iron skillet, set the heat to 'High', and add 1/4 cup oil to the skillet. Use heavy oven mitts to hold onto the skillet when necessary. Keep the mitts on while making roux, and wear an apron, in case of splashes. If you get hot roux on you, you will sustain damage. Any burns should immediately be treated with ice, and cold water (but be sure to remove the roux from the stove-top, so that it doesn't catch fire). When the pain eases up a bit, dress the burn with aloe and a light wrapping. Then check your roux, put it back onto the stove and finish the job.

Using a wire whisk, whisk in the flour a little at a time until it is all mixed into a smooth thin gravy. Continue whisking. Do not stop no matter what. As you whisk, the roux will change color gradually, from white, to tan, to brown, to reddish brown, to peanut butter-colored, to milk chocolate, and finally, to coffee-colored. Coffee-colored is what you want. If the color starts changing too quickly, lift the skillet off the burner and continue whisking until you get control of it again. Just before the color is right, carry the whole skillet over to the cooker, and carefully (it will make lots of steam, so don't put your hands or your face directly over the pot while doing this), pour the roux into the gumbo. Set the skillet in a safe place to cool (in the oven is a good place, so no one will inadvertently grab it, or touch the hot skillet...), and turn off the stove burner. Never run cold water on a hot iron skillet. it will make it warp, and ruin it.

Give the gumbo a good stir, put on the lid, seal the vent, and set the timer to 10 minutes. When the time is up, let the pressure reduce naturally.

Serve over cooked white rice with lots of fresh cornbread.

Laissez les bon temps roulet !
(Cajun for "Let the good times roll!)

Chicken Campeche

A wonderfully spicy, cheesy chicken dish in the style of Southern Mexican Cuisine.

- 2 large skinless, boneless chicken breast fillets
- 2 cups water
- 1/4 block of Velveta Queso Blanco Cheese
- 8-10 drops Mesquite Liquid Smoke
- 1/3 cup, + 4 tbsp. salsa
- Salt and pepper to taste.

Warm up the cooker.

Add water, Liquid Smoke, and 4 tbsp. salsa. Drop the chicken breasts in, lock the lid, seal

the vent and set the timer for 12 minutes if the chicken is frozen, or 8 minutes if it is thawed.

When timer is done, release pressure and remove chicken. Pour up the remaining liquid and save it for use in other recipes.

Cut chicken into 1/4" cubes and return to the cooker. Set cooker to heat.

Add a small splash of water to the bottom of the pot to keep cheese from sticking and burning.

Add cheese, the rest of the salsa, and salt and pepper to taste. Stir until the cheese is well melted and the chicken is coated.

Serve over Mexican Rice

Chicken with Blueberry Drizzle

Mouth-watering, moist, tender chicken fillets, with a delicious blueberry sauce, and a side of steamed zucchini. Out of the ordinary, and a cut above. Your taste-buds won't know what hit them.

For the sauce:

- 1/2 cup blueberry jam (sugar-free, or all-natural is OK)
- 1 tbsp. Agave Nectar (or honey)
- 1 clove garlic, crushed (or 2 tsp. garlic powder)
- 1 tsp apple cider vinegar
- 1/2 tsp. salt
- 1/2 tsp. pepper
- 1/2 tsp. Pecan, or Mesquite liquid smoke

For the Chicken:

- 2 cups water
- 4 large boneless, skinless chicken breast fillets
- 2 pounds zucchini (or similar vegetable, such as squash, broccoli, carrots, potatoes, corn-on-the-cob, etc....), cut into large chunks
- 1 tbsp. butter or margarine
- Salt and pepper to taste
- 4 squares of foil, large enough to wrap each fillet in

In a small mixing bowl, whisk all the sauce ingredients together until well mixed, and set aside. Add the water, zucchini, butter, and a little salt and pepper to the pressure cooker.

Lay out the 4 squares of foil, dull-side up, and spray with a non-stick cooking spray, or oil. Lay each breast fillet in the center of each foil square.

Lightly salt and pepper each side of the fillets, and drizzle a little sauce over each one, on both sides. Be sure to reserve at least half of the sauce.

Roll each fillet up tightly in the foil, and seal the ends by folding them up, on the seam side. Place the fillets on top of the zucchini, seam-side up.

Put the lid on the pot and lock it, and seal the pressure valve. Set the timer for 12 minutes.

When the light goes to 'Warm', you can carefully release the pressure manually if you want, or let it reduce on its own.

Remove the fillets and carefully unwrap them (they will be hot). Discard the foil.

Arrange the fillets, one to a plate, and spoon zucchini on the side. Place a dollop of butter or margarine on the zucchini, and drizzle a small amount of the blueberry sauce over each fillet.

Serve with chilled Black Bean Salad

Enjoy!

Basic Chicken Noodle Soup

A simple, wholesome American standard, and still great comfort food.

- 4 cups water
- 2 large chicken breasts (or 2 lbs. of any other kind of chicken)
- 1 small bag of noodles, or 1/2 lb. of spaghetti
- 1/2 onion, chopped
- 2 ribs celery, chopped
- 2 carrots, chopped fine or shredded
- 2 cloves garlic, minced
- 2 tbsp. oil, butter or margarine
- 1 tbsp. salt
- 2 tsp. black pepper
- 1 tsp. thyme
- 2 bay leaves

If you already have some cooked, or canned chicken, omit the first step. Set the pressure cooker to heat. Add the oil and allow to heat.

Add onions, celery, carrots and garlic and sauté until the onions are transparent.

Add water and chicken. Close and lock lid and set the timer for 15 minutes (if chicken is frozen, set to 20 minutes).

When time is up, reduce pressure, open the lid and remove chicken.

As soon as chicken can be handled, shred it and return it to the pot. Add noodles, salt, pepper, thyme, bay leaves. Close and lock the lid, and set timer for 6 minutes.

When time is up, reduce pressure manually, or naturally. Remove bay leaves. Serve with crackers and a side-salad.

Varitations:
Substitute rice for the noodles and set timer for rice, to make chicken rice soup. Substitute turkey for the chicken.

Add lemon juice for Lemon-Chicken soup.

Add basil and oregano (or Italian Seasoning) to make Italian Chicken Soup

Add broccoli, cauliflower, and/or Brussels sprouts to make Vegetable Chicken Soup

Add barley to make it even heartier.

Coconut Chicken

A Chinese Buffet favorite. Adapted for the pressure cooker.

- 2 cups water
- 4 large boneless, skinless chicken breast fillets
- 2 cans of Coconut Crème
- 2 onions, chopped
- 3 cloves garlic, minced
- 1 tbsp. lemon juice
- 1 tbsp. soy sauce
- 1 tsp. ginger
- 1 tsp. chili powder
- Salt and pepper to taste
- Add few sprigs fresh cilantro for garnish

Plug in the pressure cooker, set to heat, add oil

Add onions and garlic. Sauté until onions are translucent.

Add water, soy sauce, lemon juice, ginger, chicken, chili powder, salt and pepper. Close and lock the lid, seal the vent and set timer for 10 minutes.

When timer is done, reduce pressure. Open the lid and remove the chicken. When you can handle the chicken, cut into 1" cubes and return it to the pot.

Add coconut creme to the pot, set timer for 15 minutes and stir until chicken is well coated. Continue to cook until desired thickness is attained, stirring constantly to avoid scorching the coconut creme.

Garnish with shredded fresh cilantro, or fresh mint leaves. Serve with Fried Rice, or Coconut Rice, and egg rolls.

Cooking in Parchment (en Papillote)

Cooking with parchment in your pressure cooker is a wonderful way to prepare foods, especially delicate foods such as fish, some vegetables, and even chicken. The food steams in its own juices, and comes out melt-in-your-mouth, tender.

Many may ask, "Why wrap it in parchment? Doesn't a pressure cooker make steam?" It's a good question. It has to do with the way pressure cookers work. Since the steam cannot escape, it build up pressure (hence the name, pressure-cooker). As we said before in the 'How It Works' chapter, the pressure allows the water and steam to achieve a higher temperature than the normal 212°F at 1 atmosphere of pressure. That's one reason why the food cooks so much quicker. But it comes at a price. The environment inside a 15 psi pressure cooker is very turbulent and violent. For most foods, it's not a problem, but delicate morsels like fish would quickly succumb, and turn to mush. The way to get around that is to wrap the fish with a layer of paper. This protects the tissues from direct contact with the super-heated steam, and also holds in all the juices. The result is unbelievable. You can also use foil but don't seal to tight.

This is a very easy technique, once you get used to it. For this demonstration, I am using a steak, cut from a London Broil, because I was hungry for a steak, and they are superb fixed like this. The steps work for any kind of meat or vegetable. Here are the steps:

1. Set up your pressure cooker and add 2 cups water (or whatever liquid you want to use, to the bottom. Add any potatoes, carrots, celery, etc. you want, to the bottom and set the rack on top. In this case, I am adding beer to the liquid, just because I happen to have had one open (writing makes me thirsty...), and to show how fool-proof this is. You can also use tea, juice, wine, liquor, coffee, soda, stock...any water-based liquid, as long as it is non-dairy.

And just to show how really ridiculous you can get, and still be successful, I've added the juice from the mushrooms as well, because it was there, and I hate to waste anything.

So this is how it looks, so far....

2. Prepare your meat or vegetables however you want. I would advise leaving just a little bit of fat on cuts of meat, because that's where all the flavor is... This technique works on just about anything...and to prove it, I am not even going to use a recipe. I'll make it up as I go..... This London Broil is a bit big for a steak (even for me), so we'll start by cutting in two pieces.

Next, I'll just 'butterfly' it by cutting through it laterally, and leaving a bit attached at the center (a good kitchen knife is essential for any food preparation. This is my Cold Steel Western Hunter, possibly the greatest utility knife ever made. Make sure you get the best quality knives you can find).

Now, that's what I call a steak!

2. Cut a sheet of parchment paper at least 2-1/2 times the width of the food. Also, make sure it is long enough to fold up the ends. Lay the steak on the paper. Drizzle oil, lemon/lime juice, melted butter, margarine, olive oil, wine, or whatever you want. Just splash a bit on. It doesn't take much.

3. Sprinkle on your dry spices, such as garlic, tarragon, basil, etc....don't forget salt and pepper to taste. I'm just using a little Garlic Powder, salt and pepper here.

6. Flip the food over and repeat on that side. I added a little Worcestershire just because the bottle was handy.

7. Now, add your onions, green/jalapeño/poblano peppers, celery, carrots, mushrooms, etc.... It looks good enough to eat right now, doesn't it?

8. Carefully fold one side of the paper completely over the steak.

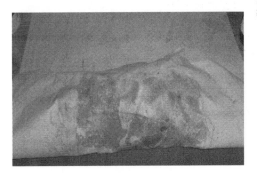

9. Make another fold, being sure the food is completely enclosed.

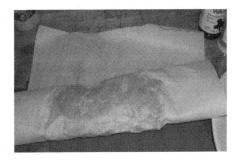

Keep going until you hit the end of the paper. Finish with the seam-side up, and the veggies on top.

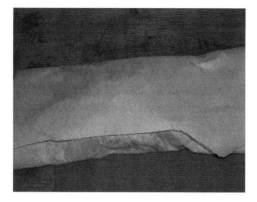

10. Fold the ends down, and under on the non-seam side. Repeat for the other pieces (if any). Here's the left side....

....and the right side. It's almost like making a paper burrito.

11. Place the food packet on the rack, seam side up, with the folds down and under. The weight of the food will keep it sealed.

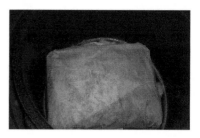

12. Put on the lid, lock it down, set the vent to 'SEAL', and set the timer for whatever you are cooking. Be sure to refer to the chart if you are not sure. If you cook it a little longer, it won't hurt with this method. Nothing can go anywhere. I am setting this for 10 minutes. When time is up, let the pressure drop normally, or you can release it manually, if you wish.

14. Carefully remove the food packets to a plate. You can either unwrap them completely, or I recommend just cutting the packets open across the top. Serving them in the packets retains all the juices, and concentrates the aromas (and it looks really neat...). They are incredible served this way. Now, just add the rest of your cooked veggies to the plate, and enjoy......

Like I said, about as fool-proof as cooking gets. This is my favorite way of cooking all fish, especially carp. Feel free to use your imagination. For a real treat, try using pork chops with a little Liquid Smoke in the liquid. They taste like they were smoked outside...honest.

Bon apetit.

Cream of Tomato Soup

For comfort food, nothing makes you feel as warm and fuzzy as a grilled cheese sandwich and a hot cup of rich Cream of Tomato soup. This is a super-easy recipe, using canned tomatoes. You can substitute fresh ones if you want. You can't hardly make this wrong.

- 1 6-lb. can of stewed tomatoes (or 6 lbs fresh), juice and all
- 2 cups stock, or water
- 1 can evaporated or filled milk
- 1 tbsp. garlic powder
- 1 tbsp. onion powder
- 1 tbsp. sugar, or Splenda (or Agave nectar)
- 2 tsp. basil
- Salt and pepper to taste

Fire up the cooker and add the stock, tomatoes, spices, sugar, salt and pepper.

Put on the lid, seal the vent and set the timer for 15 minutes.

When time is up, you can release pressure manually, or naturally. Open the lid.

Add the evaporated milk. Use an immersion blender, or ladle into a regular blender, and puree until creamy smooth.

Ladle into cups, and sprinkle a little basil, or parsley on top just before serving. Serve with grilled cheese sandwiches and pickle slices. Animus facit nobilem....

Creamy Potato Soup

A delicious wintertime favorite. You can use fresh potatoes, canned, frozen, or even leftover French Fries. They all work.

- 6 cups stock or water
- 3-4 lbs. potatoes, peeled and cubed
- 1 can Evaporated or Filled milk
- Approx. 2 cups instant mashed potato flakes
- 1/4 onion, diced
- 3 cloves garlic, minced
- 1 Tbsp. butter or Margarine
- 1 sliver fatback, bacon or salt pork, diced
- Salt and pepper to taste

Fire up the cooker. Add fatback and allow to fry until it renders some oil. Add a little olive oil if needed.

Add onions and garlic to the oil and sauté until the onions are translucent.

Add stock, potatoes, salt and pepper. Close and lock the lid, seal the vent and set timer for 15 minutes.

When the time is up, allow pressure to reduce naturally. Stir in milk and butter. With the lid off,

set timer for 20 minutes and allow the liquid to reach simmering temperatures. Using a whisk, slowly add the potato flakes a little at a time, whisking to mix evenly, until the desired thickness is achieved.

Serve in bowls and garnish with bacon bits, and shredded cheese, if you like. This spud's for you.........

Faux Baked Beans

The delicious taste of perfect baked beans, without baking, and in only 40 minutes.

- 4 cups water
- 2 cups dried navy beans
- 3/4 cup BBQ Sauce
- 1/2 cup brown sugar
- 1/2 onion, chopped
- 1 large green or poblano pepper, chopped
- 3 slices salt pork or bacon
- 4 cloves garlic, minced
- 2 tbsp Maple Syrup
- 6-10 drops Mesquite Liquid Smoke
- Salt and pepper to taste

Turn on the cooker, and set the timer for 30 minutes. Let it get hot. Fry salt pork in the bottom of the pan, until crisp. Remove and dice.

Drop onions, peppers and garlic into the salt pork drippings and sauté until the onion is translucent.

Add water, beans and diced salt pork. Lock the lid on, and close the vent. When timer is done, you can vent pressure manually, or naturally.

Remove lid and check beans. If they need more time, replace lid, and reset timer for another 10 minutes or so. Otherwise, leave the lid off, reset timer for 10 minutes and add the rest of the ingredients. Simmer, stirring occasionally until timer is finished, or until desired thickness is achieved..

These go great with BBQ pork, potato salad, and coleslaw.

Ham, Green Bean, and Potato Soup

This is my adaption of an Amish staple. I love Amish food...basic, simple, and hearty. The Amish do not use a lot of spices in their food, preferring the natural goodness of the ingredients to be expressed.

- 2 lbs. large, meaty ham bones (neck bones work well, too). Cut them with a saw if necessary to make them fit in the cooker.
- 2 quarts water
- 4 cups fresh green beans, snapped in 2" pieces (canned and frozen are OK, as well)
- 4 cups potatoes, peeled and cubed
- 1 medium onion, sliced
- 1 tbsp. dried parsley, or basil (or 1/2 tbsp. each)
- Salt and pepper to taste.

Add water and ham bones to the cooker. Close the lid, close the vent, and set the timer for 25 minutes. Allow pressure to reduce naturally.

Remove ham bones from the cooker (but leave the stock). As soon as you can, remove the meat from the bones and return it to the pot.

Add potatoes, green beans, onions, parsley/basil, and salt and pepper. Close the lid, close the vent, and set timer for 15 minutes. Allow the pressure to reduce naturally.

Serve with lots of fresh bread, rolls, biscuits or cornbread.

Meat Loaf

The most tender, delicious meat loaf you will ever eat.

* For this recipe, you will need 2 small foil bread pans. Or, you can shape the loaves by hand, and wrap them in foil, seam-side up. These are much more moist and tender than regular meatloaf, and full of flavor.

- 2 cups water + 2 tbsp.
- 1 pound hamburger meat
- 1 cup cracker crumbs
- 1 egg, beaten
- 1/2 onion, minced
- 1 clove garlic, minced
- 3 tbsp. catchup or BBQ sauce
- 1 tsp. basil
- Salt and pepper to taste
- *optional-drizzle of BBQ sauce or catchup for the tops.
- *sides: 4 Yukon Gold potatoes, or any whole potatoes that will fit in the bottom of the cooker.
- 2 cups baby carrots, or regular carrots cut into 2" pieces.

In a large mixing bowl, combine meat, egg, cracker crumbs, catchup, basil onion, garlic, salt and pepper, and 2 tbsp. of water. Mix by hand until well mixed.

Dived into 4 even pieces and press into the loaf pans (spraying them with cooking spray will help to remove loaves after cooking), or form into loaves by hand and wrap tightly with foil, seam-side up. You can put a drizzle of catchup or BBQ sauce on top, now, if desired, or wait until just before serving.

Place water, potatoes, carrots, or even corn-on-the-cob in the bottom of the pot. Set steamer rack on top of veggies (if you are not cooking veggies, then just set the rack in the bottom). Arrange loaves on rack.

Close the lid, lock it into place, close the vent and set timer for 15 minutes.

When time is up, allow pressure to reduce naturally. When pressure is reduced, open the lid, and remove the meatloaves. Replace the lid and allow the veggies to hold on 'Warm'.

Allow the meat loaves to cool for a few minutes, then carefully remove them from the pans (they should just roll right out), or unwrap them. Using a spatula, carefully place the loaves on plates. Spread catchup or BBQ sauce on top, if desired, and sprinkle with a little basil, or parsley.

Arrange veggies on plates with the loaves. Smash the potatoes with your fork and slather with lots of butter. Enjoy!

* You can omit the catchup and BBQ sauce, and instead, serve these with brown gravy drizzled over the top. Outstanding with biscuits.....

Mexican Rice

Just like the Mexican restaurants serve....

- 2 Cups water, or stock
- 2 cups Valle Verde Long Grain White Rice
- 1 cup salsa
- 2 tbsp. olive oil, butter, or margarine
- Salt and pepper to taste

Warm up the cooker

Add oil or butter and allow to heat for a minute or so.

Add rice. Stir frequently and allow it to toast until it just starts to turn beige. Add water, or stock, salsa, salt and pepper.

Lock the lid, seal the vent and set timer for 6 minutes. When timer is done, release pressure manually.

Stir the rice gently to fluff it up.

Serve with refried beans, and tortillas

Mushroom Risotto

Creamy rice with the intoxicating musky aroma of mushrooms and Parmesan cheese...a definite crowd-pleaser.

- 4 cups stock
- 2 cups arborio or Bo-Than rice
- 1 cup grated Parmesan cheese
- 1 8oz. can of mushrooms, juice and all
- 1 onion, diced
- 4 tbsp. olive oil
- 4 tbsp. butter or margarine, divided
- 2 cloves garlic, minced
- Salt and pepper to taste

Heat up the pressure cooker and add the olive oil, and 2 tbsp. of the butter. Allow it to heat for a few minutes.

Add the garlic and onions and sauté until the onions are translucent. Add the rice and stir until it is well coated with oil.

Add mushrooms, stock, salt and pepper. Close the lid and seal the vent. Set the timer for 10 minutes. When timer is done, release pressure manually. Open the lid when pressure is gone.

Stir in the remaining butter and Parmesan cheese. Serve with chicken, or fish.

Enjoy!

Navy Bean Soup

....

Wonderful Navy Bean soup that only takes 45 minutes to cook. No need to soak the beans. Just load, and forget. The natural goodness of the beans really comes through.

- 4 cups water (or chicken broth)
- 2 pounds dry navy beans, unsoaked
- 2 ribs celery, diced fine
- 1 carrot, diced fine
- 1/2 cup onion, diced fine
- 1/4 cup green pepper, diced
- 1 clove garlic, diced fine
- 1 tsp. basil
- 2 slices salt pork, or ham hock, diced fine
- 2 or 3 bay leaves
- Salt and pepper to taste

Rinse your beans well, and examine them for any bad ones, rocks, or anything that doesn't look right. Discard anything that doesn't look like a good navy bean.

Plug in the pressure cooker, set the timer for 30 minutes, and add the salt pork to the pot. Allow to cook until it makes a little oil, then add the garlic, onions, peppers, celery, and carrot. Sauté until everything is tender.

Add water, beans, basil, bay leaves, and salt and pepper.

Place lid on cooker and lock. Seal the pressure valve/ then go watch TV, or whatever. When the light goes to 'Warm', allow the pressure to reduce on its own.

Serve with cornbread, or a nice sandwich.

New England Fisherman's Dinner

Incredibly succulent fish fillets with delicious tender potatoes, and a silky-smooth white sauce. The fish is actually poaching in its own juices. Food doesn't get much better than this. You'll need some parchment paper (see technique in Pressure Cooking 101 section).

- 2 cups water
- 4 nice, large fish fillets, preferably something with white, flaky meat. I use carp, striped bass, salt cod
- (baccalao), and haddock, but just about any fish will work.
- 10-12 whole red potatoes, or 4-6 small whole Yukon Golds
- 2 tbsp. melted butter, margarine, or olive oil
- approx. 1 tbsp. garlic powder
- 2-3 tbsp. of your favorite spices, like Old Bay, basil, parsley or anything mild.
- 1 tsp. onion powder
- A few drops of lemon juice on each fillet
- Salt and pepper to taste

Sauce

- 3 tbsp. butter, margarine or oil
- 1/4 cup flour
- 2 cups milk
- Salt and pepper to taste

Cut 4 squares of parchment paper large enough to wrap fillets in.

Set a fillet on each piece of pepper and drizzle with butter, lemon juice and spices. Flip the fillets over and repeat for the other side.

Wrap the fillets (burrito-style) and set aside, seam-side down.

Plug in the pressure cooker, line the bottom with potatoes and add water. Place steamer rack on top of potatoes.

Arrange fillet packets on rack, seam-side down.

Close and lock the lid, close the vent and set timer for 10 minutes.

While fish a potatoes are cooking, place a large skillet on the stove on medium-high heat. To the skillet, add butter, or oil. Allow to melt/heat for a few minutes.

Using a whisk, add flour a tbsp. at a time, and whisk until smooth. Allow to cook for about 2 minutes, whisking constantly. You do not want the flour to brown at all. If it starts to change color, add milk immediately.

Add the milk to the flour mixture and continue to whisk until a medium thick, silky texture is achieved. Add more milk if it gets too thick. You want it about the thickness of thin pancake batter. When it's done, remove from heat.

By this time, the fish should be ready. Release the pressure manually (if it hasn't reduced on its own by now), open the lid and carefully remove the rack with the fish. Gently unwrap the fish fillets and turn them out onto the plates. Arrange the potatoes around the fillets.

Drizzle the white sauce over the fish, and the potatoes. Serve with tomato slices, or a side salad.

Variations: You can also serve this with steamed veggies, like carrots, and broccoli. Cole Slaw makes a really nice side-dish, as well.

Perfect Pinto Beans

Pressure cooked beans are the best! No need to pre-soak them. And you don't need a lot of spice. Just simple, hearty beans with their own natural flavor. This recipe works with any dried beans. Just adjust the cooking times for the type of bean you are cooking.

Pictured with a sausage sandwich on home-baked bread.

- 3 cups dried pinto beans
- 1 tsp. salt
- 1 tsp. black pepper

Water, enough to cover the beans with 2"

Go over your beans and discard any that are off-color. Remove any rocks or debris. Rinse them under cold water to remove any dirt, and/or insecticides.

Place the beans in the cooker, cover with water and add salt and pepper to taste. Set the timer for 30 minute, lock the lid and seal the vent.

When timer is done, allow the pressure to reduce naturally. Enjoy!

Pork and Beans

You'll never go back to the canned stuff again.......

- 6 cups water
- 2 cup white beans
- 1 cup tomato sauce
- 1 pork neck bone, or 3 slices salt pork, cubed
- 1 tbsp. garlic powder, or 4 cloves garlic, crushed
- 1 tbsp. onion powder, or 1 onion, diced
- 4 bay leaves
- 3 tsp. mustard
- 2 tbsp. sugar or molasses (or Splenda)
- Salt and pepper to taste

Heat up the cooker and drop in the salt pork. Let it fry until it makes some grease.

If using onions and garlic, add it to the pot and let fry in the pork fat until the onions are translucent. Add the rest of the ingredients, put on the lid, seal the vent and set timer for 40 minutes.

When the timer is done, allow pressure to reduce naturally. Serve with hot dogs, barbecue and/or potato salad.

Potato Salad

It *just wouldn't be a picnic or barbecue without potato salad. Long a staple in American Cuisine, there are as many variations of Potato Salad as there are people. This is just a generic recipe that you can tailor to your own tastes. It's as easy as Potato Salad gets.*

A couple of pounds of potatoes, washed. You can peel and cube them if you want, or cook them whole. They can be any kind of potato, red, white, Russet, or whatever.

- 2 cups water
- 1 tsp. of salt, in the water.
- 1 tsp. of oil (I prefer Olive Oil) in the water, to prevent foaming.
- 2 stalks celery, diced
- 1/2 onion, diced
- *optional-green peppers, jalapeños, boiled eggs, spices, bacon bits, etc...
- 1/3 cup mayonnaise, mustard, or any combination
- Salt and pepper to taste

Place water, potatoes, salt and oil in the cooker. Lock the lid on, seal the valve, and set the timer for about 6 minutes or so.

While the potatoes (taters, where I live...) are cooking, dice the vegetables.

When the timer is done, you can release the pressure manually, or let it go down on its own. However you decide, when the pressure is gone, open the lid and pour the potatoes in a colander (you can reserve the liquid if you want. potato water has wonderful medicinal properties...).

You can let the potatoes cool, or rinse them in cold water until you can handle them. When you can handle them, cut them in chunks for chunky salad, or mash them for country-style. You can peel them, or not. I personally like the peeling on, and mash half, and leave half chunky.

Add celery, onions, and all the other ingredients you want, and mix well. Chill for a least 3 hours before serving.

Enjoy!

Pressure Cooker Rice Pudding

The most delicious, creamy, old-fashioned rice pudding you've ever eaten.

- 2 cups milk (evaporated is OK)
- 1 cup long grain white rice
- 1 cup water
- 1 egg, beaten
- 1/3 cup tablespoons sugar (or sucralose, or agave nectar)
- 1/4 cup cream or evaporated milk
- 1 tbsp butter, or margarine
- 1/2 t salt
- 1/2 teaspoon vanilla

Warm up the pressure cooker.

Melt butter in the cooker and add rice. Allow the rice to sauté for a few minutes, stirring a few times.. Add sugar, milk, water and salt.

Set the timer for 20 minutes.

While the rice is cooking, in a mixing bowl, beat the egg with the cream or evaporated milk, and the vanilla. When the timer is done allow pressure to reduce naturally.

When pressure is released, open the lid, and set the timer for another 10 minutes.

Add the egg mixture, a little at a time, stirring vigorously until everything is all mixed together. Allow it to continue cooking until it is nice and bubbly.

Let cool slightly, serve it in small bowls, and dust with cinnamon or nutmeg. A dollop of whipped cream or Cool Whip is a nice touch.

Bon apetit.

Salisbury Steak

Delicious, tender, moist ground beef swimming in a rich gravy......

Salisbury Steak in a pressure cooker is much more flavorful and tender than when it is made in the oven. It is also much easier. This is a very basic version. Modify it as you wish, but remember, you don't need a lot of spice in a pressure cooker, so go easy. Be sure to read the section on the two-stage cooking method so you will be familiar with the technique. This is a great recipe to practice it on.

- 2 lbs. ground beef, chuck, ground round, or ground sirloin
- 2 cups water
- 1 egg, beaten
- 1 packet (or 2 cups equivalent) brown gravy mix
- 1 can mushroom slices or pieces (or 2 oz. fresh, sautéed)
- 1/4 onion, diced
- 1 tsp. garlic powder
- Salt and pepper to taste.

Warm up your pressure cooker and add 2 cups water. Allow to heat to simmering.

While the water is heating, in a mixing bowl, mix ground beef, egg, garlic, onion, salt and pepper until well mixed. Add a little water if needed.

Form the meat into palm-sized, egg-shaped ovals and set aside.

When the water begins to simmer, add gravy mix (or make brown gravy however you wish) and simmer until slightly thickened. You want it just a little thinner than normal. Add mushrooms and stir.

Gently, using a slotted spoon, place the meat ovals in the gravy. It's OK to stack them if needed. Lock on the lid, close the seal and set timer for 15 minutes. Allow pressure to reduce naturally.

Using a slotted wooden or plastic spoon, gently remove the meat ovals to plates, and ladle the gravy over the top. Serve with rice, or mashed potatoes, and peas.

Salmon Chowder

A delicious chowder with the great taste of mild salmon. This recipe works for almost any kind of fish, or chicken.

- 1 pound salmon fillets, skin removed (or canned salmon)
- 16 oz. of water
- 4 potatoes, peeled and diced
- 1 onion, diced
- 1 can of evaporated milk
- 1 can of corn
- 1 pt. half and half
- a splash of white wine
- 3 tbsp. olive oil
- Salt & Pepper to taste

Heat up the pressure cooker

Add the olive oil and allow it to heat up. Add the onions and sauté until they are translucent.

Add the salmon fillets and continue to sauté. When fish is done, break it up into chunks with a wooden, or plastic spoon

Splash a little white wine in the pot to de-glaze it, and allow it to evaporate. Add potatoes, water, corn, salt and pepper.

Lock the lid, close the vent and set the timer for 10 minutes. When timer is done, allow pressure to reduce naturally. Remove lid, and reset timer for 10 minutes.

Add milk, half-and half, and allow to cook until chowder is slightly thickened. Serve with coleslaw, or a side-salad, and crackers.

* If you want your chowder a little thicker and richer, you can add a little white roux at the final cooking stage.

Salmon en Papillote

This technique works with almost any kind of fish.

- 2-4 thawed salmon fillets, cut 4"-6" long, with skins removed
- 1 cup water
- *Optional-8-10 drops Liquid Smoke
- For each fillet:
- 1 tsp. olive oil, or melted butter
- 1/2 tsp. lemon juice
- 1/4 tsp. garlic powder
- 1/4 tsp. dried dill
- Salt and pepper to taste

Warm up the cooker, and add the water. For a smoked salmon taste, add 8-10 drops of Liquid Smoke to the water.

While the water is heating, prepare the salmon according to the instructions in the "Cooking In Parchment Paper" section. Place a dollop of butter or olive oil, lemon juice, garlic, salt and pepper, and dill on each fillet before wrapping.

Place the trivet in the pot, and set the salmon packets on it. Lock the lid, close the vent and set them timer for 8 minutes.

When timer is done, release pressure manually. You can remove the fish from the packets, or leave them in...your choice.

Serve with just about anything.......

the liquid for use in other recipes. It can be frozen.

Simple Split Pea Soup

. . . .

Another great winter soup

- 3 quarts vegetable stock
- 3 cups split peas
- 5 carrots, diced
- 1 large onion, diced
- Salt and pepper to taste.

Add everything to the pressure cooker, close the lid, close the vent and set timer for 20 minutes. Allow the pressure to reduce naturally.

Tamales

Succulent spicy pork wrapped in a tasty corn dough. Need I say more...?

For the filling:

- 4 cups water
- 2-3 lb. pork roast or tenderloin
- 1/4 onion, course chopped
- 3 tsp. Chili Powder
- 2 tsp. cumin
- 2 tsp. oregano
- 2 whole fresh (not pickled) jalapeño peppers

For the tamales:

- 2 dozen corn husks, soaked
- 3 cups instant masa harina mix
- approx. 2 cups of the liquid you cooked the pork in

It's best to cook the pork (called 'Carnitas') the day before you want to make the tamales. That way the meat, and liquid are cool enough to handle. Just stand guard over the carnitas (absolutely delicious by themselves...) to keep everyone out of it until you are ready to make tamales.

Start by heating up the pressure cooker. Add water, onions, garlic, chili powder, cumin, oregano, jalapeños, and the pork roast to the cooker. Close the lid, close the vent and set the timer for 45 minutes.

Ignore the incredible mouth-watering aromas coming from the kitchen. When timer is done, allow pressure to reduce naturally. Unplug the cooker, and allow the carnitas to set for an hour or so. Wash the cooker and set it back up.

Remove the meat from the cooker, and reserve the liquid in the refrigerator when it cools. Using two forks, pull the pork apart (it will literally fall apart on its own, with just a little coaxing). Remove the bone to cool (if there is one), and give it to some well-deserving dog. Chop the jalapeño and add it to the meat, or just eat it.

The next day, in the sink, soak the corn husks in cold water for 1 hour. Put 2 cups of water in the cooker, and heat it up. Place the trivet in the bottom.

In a mixing bowl, add 3 cups of the masa harnia. Add the 2 cups of the pork liquid, a little at a time, mixing until you get a medium-thick dough.

Get your pork from the refrigerator.

Gently unfold a corn husk and press a layer of masa dough onto it, covering most of the husk. Next, place a spoonful or two of the pork onto the dough. Roll the whole thing up and either fold or tie the ends shut. Place the tamale on end on the trivet in the cooker. You can lay it down on the trivet and stack them if you'd rather, but they cook better on end.

Continue with the other corn husks until you have the cooker packed, not too tightly, but enough to where the tamales stay standing up. Put the lid on, close the vent and set the timer for 20 minutes. Go ahead and make the rest of the tamales while these are cooking.

When the timer is done, release pressure manually, and carefully lever the tamales out of the cooker. Add a new batch, replace the lid, close the vent, and continue. Keep going until all the filling is used up.

The tamales can be eaten immediately, or frozen for future use.

Serve with lots of Mexican rice, refried beans and tostadas. Garnish with salsa, guacamole, and sour cream.

Ole!

The Ultimate Vegetarian Chili

This tastes even better than normal chili with meat. You can make it as hot, or as mild as you like simply by adjusting the amount of peppers you put in. This recipes makes a Texas-Medium hot chili.

- 1 qt. water
- 2-30oz. cans of Chili Beans (or equivalent of cooked beans, black, pinto, red or pink)
- 2-14.5 oz. cans crushed tomatoes (or equivalent of fresh tomatoes)
- 1-14.5 oz. can of corn (or frozen)
- 1-8 oz. can of mushrooms (or fresh ones, sautéed), diced fine
- 1 cup raw bulgar wheat
- 1 cup raw TVP
- 1/2 of a large onion, chopped
- 1/4 cup Soy Sauce
- 8 large fresh Jalepeño peppers (canned are OK, too), diced fine (you can cut back on them for milder chili, or add more for hotter. You can also cut back on the heat some by removing the seeds and veins from the peppers)
- 5 cloves of garlic, crushed
- 8 tbsp. chili powder
- 2 tbsp. ground cumin
- 1 tbsp. oregano
- 1 tbsp. olive oil
- Salt and pepper to taste

Plug in the pressure cooker, and set to heat or sauté mode. Place the olive oil in the pot and let it heat up a bit. Then add the onions, garlic and peppers, and sauté them until the onions begin to caramelize.

Add the soy sauce and allow it to simmer for 3 or 4 minutes, stirring constantly.

Add all the canned ingredients, juice and all (including the mushroom juice, and corn juice). Stir well. Add all the spices, and stir well.

Add the Bulgar Wheat and TVP, and stir well. Add salt and pepper if desired.

Add the water, up to around 3/4 full in the pot. Don't go much over this. Stir well.

Put on the lid, lock it down, and seal the pressure valve. Set the timer for 25 minutes. Allow to pot to reduce pressure naturally.

Serve with lots of salsa and tortillas, or tostada chips.

Whole Steamed Chicken

People are so used to spices these days, they have forgotten how delicious just plain chicken can be, all on its own.

You'll need to use a trivet with handles, or make handles out of folded foil, to be able to lift the bird out of the cooker. It will fall apart very easily

- 1 whole chicken, internal parts removed (you know, the bag inside that everyone forgets sometimes....). Perdue chickens are the best, if you can find one. Cornish hens also work.
- 2 cups water
- *Optional-8-12 drops of Pecan or Mesquite Liquid Smoke
- Salt and pepper to taste
- Paprika for sprinkle

Warm up the cooker.

Add water. Place the trivet in the cooker. Add Liquid Smoke to the water, if desired. Place chicken on trivet

Lock the lid, close the seal and set timer for 30 minutes for a 5 lb. bird. A bit more for a larger bird, a bit less for a smaller one.

When timer is done, allow pressure to reduce naturally.

Carefully ease the trivet, with the bird on it, out of the cooker. Slide the whole bird onto a carving platter. Save the liquid for use in other recipes.

Serve with cranberry sauce, rice, and green peas.

Appendix II
Extra Recipes

MEAT

Apple Pork Loin Chops

Ingredients

- 4 thick pork loin chops
- 2 lbs. sauerkraut, rinsed, drained, and squeezed dry
- 2 Tbs. vegetable oil
- 1/2 teaspoon salt
- 1/4 teaspoon black pepper
- 3 medium-sized sweet potatoes peeled and cut into 2-inch chunks
- 3 red delicious apples, peeled, cored, and cut in half
- 1/2 cup apple juice
- 1/2 cup packed light brown sugar
- 2 tsp. ground cinnamon

Procedure

Season chops with salt and pepper. Set the pressure cooker to heat or sauté. Add the oil to heat.

Add 2 chops at a time to the pressure cooker and brown on both sides. Remove all 4 chops to a plate.

Place sweet potatoes in bottom of cooker. Layer pork chops and apples over them.

In a bowl combine apple juice, brown sugar, and cinnamon. Mix well and pour over the chops.

Top with sauerkraut. Close and lock the lid. Seal the pressure valve. Set the timer for 15 minutes.

When done wait 10 minutes then release the pressure manually. Serve on a platter, ladle sauce over all.

Beef Brisket

Ingredients

- 1 brisket 4 to 5 pounds
- 2 cups thinly sliced Spanish onion
- 1 cup peeled, coarsely chopped carrots
- 1 cup chopped celery
- 1 cup grain mustard
- 2 envelops Lipton's onion soup mix
- ⅓ cup Worcestershire sauce
- ⅓ cup red or white wine
- ⅓ cup canola oil
- ¼ cup minced flat-leaf parsley leaves
- 5 cloves garlic, minced
- 2 bay leaves
- Kosher salt
- Freshly ground black pepper

Procedures

Set the pressure cooker to heat or sauté and add the oil.

Season brisket with salt and pepper.

When the oil is hot sear the brisket on all sides until brown.

Remove brisket and add onions, carrots, celery, garlic, and bay leaves.

Spread mustard on brisket. Sprinkle onion soup mix on each side.

Place brisket back in the pressure cooker fat side up on top of vegetables.

Top with remaining vegetables.

Pour wine and Worcestershire sauce over meat and vegetables.

Close and lock lid. Seal the pressure valve. Set the timer for 45 minutes.

When the cooking time is done let pressure release naturally.

Remove the brisket to a platter

Remove sauce from cooker into foil tray.

Place brisket into sauce and vegetables in tray and cover with foil

Place in oven at 325 degrees for 10 minutes and serve hot

Carnitas

Ingredients

- 4 lbs. boneless pork shoulder/rump roast
- 2 tsp. salt
- 2 tsp garlic powder
- 2 tsp. gr cumin
- 1 tsp crumbled dried oregano
- 1 tsp gr coriander
- 1/2 tsp. ground cinnamon
- 2 bay leaves
- 2 Serrano Peppers, chopped
- 2 small chili peppers
- 2 cups chicken broth

Procedure

Mix all the dry spice ingredients, except for the Chiles and bay leaves in a bowl.

Rub the roast with the mixture. Add a trivet to the pressure cooker and set the roast on it.

Pour chicken stock, chopped Serrano peppers, and bay leaves over the roast into the cooker.

Close and lock the lid. Seal the pressure valve. Set the timer for 45 minutes.

When the time is up release the pressure manually.

Remove the roast and trivet and replace the roast in the liquid.

Set the timer for 10 additional minutes with lid locked and the pressure sealed.

When the time is up release the pressure naturally and serve or shred into pieces for carnitas

Herbed Lamb

Ingredients

- 4 lbs. boneless lamb, cubed
- Salt and pepper
- 2 Tbs. olive oil
- 4 cloves of garlic, minced
- 3 Tbs. flour
- 1 1/2 cups vegetable stock
- 4 pieces of fresh rosemary
- 1 cup thickly sliced carrots

Procedure

Season lamb cubes with salt and pepper.

Heat olive oil in the open pressure cooker in the heat or sauté mode.

Add lamb and garlic. Brown the lamb on all sides. Pour in the stock.

Add the carrots and rosemary. Close and lock the lid. Seal the pressure valve.

Set the timer for 20 minutes. When the cooking time is up release the pressure naturally.

Remove herb stems. Serve warm

Latin Pork Loin with Vegetables

Ingredients

- 2 lbs. boneless pork loin
- 4 to 6 small cloves garlic
- Salt and freshly ground black pepper, to taste
- 2 Tbs. oil, olive or veg.
- 2 cups water
- 1 bay leaf
- 1 medium onion cut in quarters
- 3 carrots cut in 2" pieces
- 3 stalks of celery cut in 2" pieces
- 3 medium potatoes quartered
- 3 Tbs. butter or olive oil

Procedure

With a knife, cut 1/2" deep slits in pork about one inch apart. Alternately insert garlic cloves and onion slivers.

Season with salt and pepper. Heat the oil in the pressure cooker on the heat or sauté mode.

Cook the meat in heated oil to brown on all sides. Carefully add water not to exceed 2/3 mark.

Close and lock the lid. Seal the pressure valve. Set the timer for 40 minutes. When the cooking time is up release the pressure manually and remove the meat.

Place a trivet in the pressure cooker. Place potatoes and vegetables on the rack. Place meat on top of vegetables. Close lid and lock, seal the pressure valve and set the timer for another 10 minutes. Release the pressure natually. Remove and Rest the meat for 5 minutes before slicing. Serve with the cooked vegetables.

Pork Sandwiches

Ingredients

- 3 lbs. boneless pork loin roast
- 1-1/2 tbs. sugar
- 1-1/4 cups cider vinegar
- 3/4 cup barbecue sauce, plus extra if desired
- 6 hamburger buns, toasted

Procedure

Sprinkle pork with salt and pepper to taste.

Combine pork loin, sugar, and vinegar in the pressure cooker.

Close and lock lid. Seal the pressure valve. Set the timer for 45 minutes.

When the cooking time is up release the pressure naturally.

Open the lid and place the pork in bowl to cool. Shred meat by hand or with 2 forks.

Stir in BBQ sauce to moisten. Serve on buns. Delicious with or without sauce

Pot Roast

Ingredients

- 3lb chuck roast
- 3 Tbs. olive oil
- 1 cup onion, thinly sliced
- 1 cup carrots, peeled and cut in 2" pieces
- 1 cup celery, peeled and cut into small pieces
- 2 cups beef broth
- Salt and pepper
- 2 Tbs. A1 sauce
- 2 Tbs. Worcestershire sauce
- 8 red potatoes
- 1 bay leaf

Procedure

Heat the oil in the pressure cooker in the heat or sauté mode. Season the roast well with salt & pepper.

Sear the roast on all sides in the heated olive oil. Add the onions and celery and stir for 2-3 minutes.

Add the beef broth and scrape off any brown bits on the bottom of the pan.

Add in the A1 sauce and the Worcestershire sauce and the bay leaf.

Close and lock lid. Seal the pressure valve. Set the timer for 50 minutes.

Release pressure manually when the cooking time is done. Open the lid and add the potatoes and the carrots.

Close and lock the lid and seal the pressure valve. Set the timer for 8 more minutes.

When the time is up release the pressure manually.

Open the lid, remove the roast to a platter, let cool for a few minute and slice. Serve with juices and vegetables.

Steak Roll-Ups

Ingredients

- 2 1/2 pounds round steak
- 1 cup flour
- 1 tsp salt
- 1/2 tsp pepper
- 1 cup fresh bread crumbs
- 1 small chopped onion
- 2 cups chopped butter nut squash
- 1/4 cup green pepper
- 1/4 cup chopped celery
- 1 egg
- 2 Tbs. melted butter or margarine
- 1/4 cup margarine or butter

Procedure

Cut steaks into 8 pieces 1/2-inch thick. Pound with meat mallet until 1/4 inch thick.

Combine flour, 1 teaspoon salt, and pepper. Dredge seasoned flour on each piece of meat.

Mix together bread crumbs, onion, squash, green pepper, celery, 1 teaspoon salt, beaten egg, and 2 tablespoons melted margarine.

Spread squash mixture evenly over each piece of meat, roll and fasten with a toothpick.

Brown meat rolls on all sides in 1/4 cup margarine in the cooker in the heat mode.

Remove rolls and place 1 cup water and cooking rack in the cooker. Place the rolls on the rack.

Close and lock lid. Set the timer for 15 minutes. Seal the pressure valve.

When the cooking time is up wait 10 minutes and then release the remaining pressure.

Open the lid. Remove beef rolls and drizzle with pan juice.

Sherried Beef Manhattan

Ingredients

- 3 lbs. Beef Round Steak Cubes or Stew Meat
- 8 oz. Slice Mushrooms
- 2 Cans Golden Mushroom Soup
- 1 Cup Sherry (can substitute beef broth)
- 1 Envelope Onion Soup Mix
- 1 Loaf French Bread- Sliced and Toasted
- 1 Tub Mashed Potatoes

Instructions

Add the mushroom soup, sherry, onion soup mix and mushrooms to the pressure cooker and stir.

Add the meat and mix into the liquid. Close and lock the lid. Seal the pressure valve.

Set the timer for 25 minutes. When the cooking time is done, release the pressure manually.

Top toasted bread with mashed potatoes and spoon beef and gravy over top.

Serves 6

Barbacoa Beef

Serves 6

Ingredients

- 1/3 cup apple cider vinegar
- 4 teaspoons minced garlic cloves
- 4 teaspoons cumin
- 2 teaspoons oregano
- 1 teaspoon ground black pepper
- 1 teaspoon salt
- 1/2 teaspoon ground cloves
- 3/4 cup chicken broth
- 3 tablespoons lime juice
- 3 -4 chipotle chilies in adobo
- 2 tablespoons vegetable oil
- 3 bay leaves
- 4 -5 lbs. chuck roast

Directions

Combine vinegar, garlic, cumin, oregano, pepper, salt, cloves, lime juice, and chipotle chilies in a blender until well blended.

Cut off most of the fat from the roast and then cut into big chunks (approximately 6).

Heat the oil in the pressure cooker in the heat or sauté mode. Once hot, add chunks of meat and sear on all sides.

Pour the blended sauce onto the beef. Pour in the chicken broth and add bay leaves. Close and lock the lid and set the timer for 60 minutes.

When cooking time is up let sit for 10 minutes and then release the remaining pressure manually. Open the lid. Remove meat and shred. Return to the cooker and mix, keep warm. Serve as desired.

Ginger Beef with Mandarin Oranges

Serves 4-6

Ingredients

- 2 lbs. boneless beef chuck roast
- 1 can (8 oz.) sliced water chestnuts, drained
- 1 can (11 oz.) mandarin orange sections (reserve juice)
- 1 cup thickly sliced mushrooms
- 1 small onion, sliced
- 1 cup beef stock
- 1/3 cup soy sauce
- 1 tbs. sherry or mirin
- 2 tbs. vegetable oil
- 1 tbs. grated fresh ginger -OR- 1 tsp ground ginger
- 2 tbs. cornstarch
- 3 green onions, chopped

Directions

Trim the beef of visible fat. Cut in 1/4-inch slices. Set the pressure cooker to heat or sauté.

Heat 1 tbs. of the oil in the pressure cooker. When oil just begins to smoke, add the beef slices, making sure not to overcrowd the pan. Brown well on both sides. Repeat if you had meat that you couldn't fit the first time.

Heat the rest of the oil. Add the mushrooms, water chestnuts and onion. Sauté until onion softens.

Add the soy sauce, ginger and the sherry, scraping up all the browned bits at the bottom of the pan.

Put the mushroom mixture on top of the meat in the pressure cooker. Add the beef stock.

Cover and set the timer for 25 minutes. Seal the pressure valve. When the cooking time is done wait 5 minutes then release the pressure manually.

Open the lid. Drain the mandarin orange slices. Set the drained sections aside. Mix reserved mandarin orange syrup with the cornstarch, mixing well. Add the mixture to the hot cooking liquid and stir till sauce thickens. Serve over rice.

Creamed Herbed Pork Chops

Serves 4

Ingredients

- 2 lbs. pork loin chops
- 1 tablespoon olive oil
- 1 tablespoon butter
- ½ small yellow onion, diced (or about ¼ cup)
- 2-3 cloves garlic, minced
- 1 teaspoon dried thyme
- ½ teaspoon salt
- ½ teaspoon dried mustard powder
- ⅛ (or up to ¼) teaspoon pepper, to taste
- 1½ cup chicken broth
- ¾ cup heavy cream
- 1 tablespoon cornstarch
- 1 teaspoon freeze dried parsley
- 1 teaspoon freeze dried basil

Instructions

Sprinkle each side of pork chops with thyme, salt, pepper and mustard

Melt butter with olive oil in the pressure cooker in the brown or heat mode

Add onion and garlic and sauté for about 2 minutes

Move onions and garlic to side of pressure cooker pan and add seasoned pork chops

Sauté for about 2 minutes on each side until lightly browned

Add chicken broth. Cover and set the timer for 15 minutes. Seal the pressure valve.

When the cooking time is up release the pressure manually and open the lid.

Remove pork chops and cover to keep warm

Add cream to the pressure cooker and whisk

To thicken sauce more, whisk in 1 tablespoon cornstarch. Bring to a boil on heat or simmer mode for 2-3 minutes until thickened as desired

Pour sauce over pork chops and garnish with freeze dried herbs

Pressure Cooker Country Pork Roast

Serves 6

Ingredients

- 1 (2-3 pound) pork roast
- ½ cup all-purpose flour
- 1 teaspoon seasoned salt
- 1 teaspoon onion powder
- 1 teaspoon garlic powder
- 1 teaspoon ground mustard
- ½ teaspoon dried oregano
- 2 tablespoons olive oil
- 1 can (14.5 ounce) chicken broth
- 1 lb. baby carrots (or sliced carrots- whatever you prefer)
- ¼ cup cornstarch
- ¼ cup cold water

Directions

Cut the roast in half. Place flour, seasoned salt, onion powder, garlic powder, ground mustard, and oregano in a gallon-sized Ziploc bag.

Add one half the roast to the bag, seal the bag, and shake it until the roast is entirely coated.

Repeat with the other half of the roast.

Heat olive oil in the pressure cooker in the heat mode and brown both pieces of the roast on all sides

Dump in the carrots and pour the chicken broth on top of the roast, close and lock the lid.

Set the timer for 20 minutes. When cooking time is done, wait 5 minutes then release pressure manually. Open lid.

Remove roast from pressure cooker to cutting board and slice. Using a slotted spoon, remove the carrots. To thicken sauce, mix together cornstarch and water, add to the pressure cooker and bring to a boil.

Cook for 2-3 minutes or until gravy thickens up. Serve with mashed potatoes and pour gravy on top.

Pressure Cooker Pork Chops with Golden Ranch Gravy

Ingredients

- 4 center-cut rib pork chops (bone-in or boneless)
- 1 can cream of chicken soup (10.75 oz.)
- 1 envelope ranch dressing mix
- ¼ cup water
- 1 tbs. butter

Directions

Melt butter in the pressure cooker in the heat or sauté mode.

Brown pork chops well on both sides, about 3 minutes per side.

Add the soup, water and ranch dressing together in a bowl and mix well.

Pour soup mixture over pork chops in the pressure cooker. Cover and lock the lid.

Set the timer for 10 minutes. Seal the pressure valve.

When the cooking time is up, let the pressure release naturally. Open the lid, remove and serve.

Pressure Cooker Lasagna Soup

Makes 8 Servings

Ingredients

- 1 pound Italian sausage links, cut into bite-sized pieces
- 2 large onions, diced
- 5 garlic cloves, minced
- 1 tablespoon dried oregano
- 1/4 teaspoon red pepper flakes
- 1-6 ounce can tomato paste
- 1-28 ounce can fire-roasted tomatoes
- 2 bay leaves
- 6 cups chicken broth
- Salt and pepper, to taste
- 10 ounces curly pasta (fusilli)
- Ricotta and mozzarella cheeses for topping

Directions

Combine all ingredients except pasta and cheeses. Add to pressure cooker. Place on the lid and lock it.

Turn the vent knob to seal. Set the timer for 15 minutes. When done release pressure manually.

Open the lid carefully. Add in pasta and make sure it's covered with the cooking liquid.

Close and lock the lid and seal the pressure valve. Set the timer for 5 minutes.

When the cooking time is done release the pressure manually. When ready to serve, preheat broiler.

Spoon soup into oven-proof bowls. Top each bowl with a spoon of ricotta and a sprinkling of mozzarella.

Place under the broiler for 3-5 minutes or until cheese is hot and melted.

Chinese Barbeque Pork

Ingredients

- 1/4 cup lower-sodium soy sauce
- 1/4 cup hoisin sauce
- 3 tablespoons ketchup
- 3 tablespoons honey
- 2 teaspoons minced garlic
- 2 teaspoons grated peeled fresh ginger
- 1 teaspoon dark sesame oil
- 1/2 teaspoon five-spice powder
- 1 (2-pound) boneless pork shoulder (Boston butt), trimmed
- 1/2 cup fat-free, lower-sodium chicken broth

Preparation

Combine first 8 ingredients in a small bowl, stirring well with a whisk. Place in a large zip-top plastic bag.

Add pork to the bag and seal. Marinate in the refrigerator at least 2 hours, turning occasionally.

Place pork and marinade in the electric pressure cooker. Add broth. Cover and set timer for 40 minutes. Seal the pressure valve, When the cooking time is done release thevpressure naturally. Open the lid.

Remove the pork to a cutting board and let cool for 5 minutes, then cut ½" slices. Serve with the sauce.

If the sauce is not thick enough, mix a tablespoon of corn starch with a tablespoon of water, add to cooker.

Mix and let heat till desired thickness.

PC Pork Roast with Potatoes and Carrots

Ingredients

- 1 ½ pound boneless pork loin
- 2 tablespoons of olive oil
- 4 potatoes, peeled and cut into cubes
- 3 carrots, scraped and cut into small cubes
- 1 clove crushed garlic
- Herbs to taste: thyme, rosemary, basil, marjoram, celery seed, nutmeg, parsley
- ½ cup chicken broth

Directions

Heat oil in the pressure cooker in the heat or sauté mode, then add cut up potatoes and carrots.

Cook vegetables till browned. Remove and set aside. Sear the pork loin in the pressure cooker.

Add garlic and continue cooking for one minute. Add broth and herbs.

Close and lock the lid, seal the pressure valve and set the timer for 35 minutes.

When the cooking time is up release the pressure naturally. Open the lid

Add the carrots and potatoes to the cooker. Reseal the lid and set timer for 6 minutes.

Release pressure manually when time is up. Open the lid. Slice pork thin and serve hot with vegetables.

Meatballs with Marinara Sauce

Ingredients

- 1 pound extra lean ground beef of turkey
- 1/4 cup water
- 1 tablespoon garlic, minced
- ½ teaspoon salt
- ¼ teaspoon pepper
- ½ cup instant brown rice
- 1 cup breadcrumbs
- 1/2 cup milk
- 2 tablespoons tomato paste
- 1 (24-ounce) can marinara sauce

Instructions

Combine meat, garlic, salt, pepper, rice, bread crumbs, milk and tomato paste in a bowl.

Shape into meatballs with hands or an ice cream scoop. Heat oil in the pressure cooker in the heat mode.

Place the meatballs in the cooker and brown well. When browned pour in the marinara sauce and water.

Close and lock the lid and set the timer for 15 minutes. Seal the pressure valve.

When the cooking time is done, release the pressure manually. Open the lid and serve the hot meatballs and sauce.

Low-Fat Meatballs with Mushroom Sauce

Ingredients

- 1 pound extra lean ground beef or turkey
- 1/4 cup water
- 1 cup skim milk (divided)
- ½ cup instant brown rice
- ¼ cup chopped onion
- 1 cup dry breadcrumbs
- ½ teaspoon salt
- Dash of black pepper
- 1 (10 ¾-ounce) can low-fat, low-sodium cream of mushroom soup

Instructions

Combine meat, 1/2 cup skim milk, rice, onion, bread crumbs, salt, and pepper in a bowl.

Shape into meatballs with your hands or an ice cream scoop. Place in the bottom of the pressure cooker, in a single layer.

Mix together soup and ½ cup milk. Pour over the top of the meatballs. Pour in the 1/4 cup of water.

Cover and lock the lid, seal the pressure valve and set the timer for 15 minutes.

Release the pressure manually and serve the meatballs with the mushroom soup gravy.

Pressure Cooker Hawaiian Pork

Ingredients

- 2 1/2 pounds pork, cut in 1" cubes
- 4 tablespoons oil
- 1 medium onion, sliced
- 1 1/2 cup pineapple juice
- 1/2 cup water
- 1/2 cup vinegar
- 1/2 cup brown sugar
- 1 1/2 teaspoon salt
- 1 cup green bell pepper, diced
- 2 cans (1 lb 4 ounce size) pineapple chunks
- 2 tablespoons soy sauce
- 5 tablespoons corn starch
- 1/2 cup water

Instructions

Set the pressure cooker to heat or sauté, add the oil and heat.

Brown the pork cubes and onion slices in hot oil.

Add pineapple juice, water, vinegar, brown sugar and salt.

Cover, seal the pressure valve and set the timer for 10 minutes.

When the cooking time is done reduce pressure manually and open the lid.

Add diced green pepper, pineapple chunks and soy sauce and stir. Add corn starch mixed with water and cook on heat until thickened, stirring constantly. Serve over rice.

Best Pressure Cooker Pork Chops

Ingredients

- 8 pork chops, cut 1/2 inch thick
- 2 tablespoons oil
- 2 cups rice, uncooked
- 4 cups tomatoes, canned
- 2 teaspoons salt
- 1/2 teaspoon black pepper
- 1/2 teaspoon chili powder
- 4 tablespoons onion, chopped
- 6 tablespoons green bell pepper, chopped
- 2 cups water

Directions

Set the pressure cooker to heat or sauté and add the oil.

Brown the pork chops well on both sides, two at a time then remove and set aside.

Place rice in the hot oil. Stir until browned. Add the tomatoes, seasonings, chopped onion and green pepper. Pour in the water and stir well.

Add thevpork chops to the pressure cooker.

Cover and lock the lid, seal the pressure valve and set the timer for 12 minutes.

When the cooking time is up release the pressure naturally, open the lid and remove the pork chops.

Stir the rice mixture till done to your liking and serve with the pork chops.

Pressure Cooker Pot Roast with Vegetables

Ingredients

- 3 pounds boneless beef sirloin tip roast
- 2 tablespoons vegetable oil
- 4 large potatoes, peeled and quartered
- 4 large carrots, cut into 2-inch pieces
- 1 large onion, cut into wedges
- 2 cups water
- 1 teaspoon beef bouillon granules
- 1/2 teaspoon salt
- 1/4 teaspoon black pepper
- 3 tablespoons corn starch
- 3 tablespoons cold water

Directions

Heat the oil in the pressure cooker set on salute or heat. Season the roast with salt and pepper.

Brown the roast in oil on all sides in the pressure cooker. Add the onion and broth.

Close and lock the lid, seal the pressure valve and set the timer for 40 minutes.

When the pressure cooking time is up release the pressure naturally. Open the lid.

Remove meat and keep warm. Add the potatoes and carrots.

close and lock the lid and seal the pressure valve.

Set the timer for 5 minutes. When done release the pressure manually. Open the lid.

Combine the corn starch and cold water until smooth; stir into juices.

Cook and stir for 2 minutes or until thickened. Slice the roast and serve with sauce and vegetables.

Pressure Cooker One Pot Spaghetti and Meat Sauce

Ingredients

- 2 tablespoons olive oil
- 1 pound ground beef
- 1 cup chopped onion
- 1 clove garlic, mashed
- 2 cans (8 ounce size) tomato sauce
- 2 cups dry red wine
- 1 1/2 cups water
- 1 pound spaghetti pasta, uncooked
- 1 1/2 teaspoon chili powder
- 1 1/2 teaspoon salt
- 1/4 cup grated Parmesan cheese

Directions

Set the pressure cooker to heat or sauté and add oil.

Lightly brown ground beef, onion and garlic, stirring occasionally to separate meat.

Add the tomato sauce, red wine, and water.

Add uncooked pasta into liquid so it separates and is just covered (if spaghetti is to long break strands in half before adding).

Close and lock cover and set the timer for 8 minutes. Seal the pressure valve.

When the pressure cooking time is up release the pressure manually and remove lid.

Stir cheese into mixture before serving.

Pressure Cooker Cola Braised Short Ribs

Ingredients

- 2 teaspoons kosher salt
- 2 teaspoons paprika
- 1 1/2 teaspoons freshly ground black pepper
- 1 1/2 teaspoons cayenne pepper
- 1/2 teaspoon ground cumin
- 4 to 5 pounds English-cut beef short ribs, cut crosswise into 2-1/2-inch-long pieces
- 2 tablespoons olive oil
- 6 medium garlic cloves, peeled and smashed
- 1/2 medium yellow onion, small dice
- 2 cups cola (not diet), such as Coca-Cola
- 2 tablespoons soy sauce
- 2 tablespoons Worcestershire sauce
- 2 tablespoons corn starch
- 2 tablespoons water

Instructions

Combine the salt, paprika, black pepper, cayenne, and cumin in a small bowl.

Evenly rub the spice mix on all sides of the ribs; set aside.

Heat the oil in the electric pressure cooker in the heat or sauté mode. Add enough short ribs to cover the bottom of the cooker without crowding them.

Sear, turning occasionally, until the ribs are browned on all sides, about 6 minutes.

Transfer to a large plate and repeat with the remaining ribs till all the ribs are browned on the plate.

Add the garlic and onion and cook, stirring occasionally, until softened, about 4 minutes.

Add the cola, soy sauce, and Worcestershire and, using large spoon, scrape up the browned bits from the bottom of the pressure cooker.

Return the ribs to the pressure cooker, turn to coat them in the sauce, and lock the lid in place.

Set the timer for 30 minutes. Meanwhile, set a strainer over a large bowl; set aside. When the cooking time is up release the pressure naturally.

Transfer the ribs to a large plate and set aside. Pour the liquid through the strainer and return the contents of the strainer to the pressure cooker. Using a large spoon, skim off and discard the fat from the strained liquid and return the liquid to the pressure cooker (alternatively you can use a fat separator).

Return the pressure cooker to the heat mode and bring the mixture to a boil. Place the corn starch and water in a small bowl, whisk to combine, and add half of the mixture to the pressure cooker. Cook, whisking constantly, until the sauce is glossy and thickened, about 30 seconds (add more corn starch mixture as necessary if you want a thicker sauce). Turn off the heat, spoon sauce over the ribs. Serve immediately.

Pressure Cooker Hamburger Casserole

Ingredients

- 1 1/2 pounds ground beef
- 2 large potatoes, sliced
- 2 or 3 medium carrots, sliced
- 1 can peas
- 2 medium onions sliced
- Salt & pepper to taste
- 2 stalks celery, sliced
- 1 can tomato soup
- 1/2 can water

Directions:

Add potatoes, carrots, onion, celery and peas to the pressure cooker

Cover with water and tomato soup.

Add the beef and spices and mix together.

Close and lock the lid and make sure pressure valve is sealed. Set the timer for 18 minutes.

When the time is up, release the pressure manually. Remove the lid and sprinkle top with cheddar cheese.

Beef with Broccoli

Ingredients:

- 1 lb. boneless, beef chuck roast, sliced into thin strips
- 1 cup beef stock or beef broth
- 1/2 cup low sodium soy sauce
- 1/3 cup dark brown sugar
- 1 tbsp. sesame oil
- 3 garlic cloves minced
- 2 tbsp. corn starch
- Frozen Broccoli Florets (one bag)
- White or brown rice, cooked

Directions:

In a mixing bowl, whisk together the beef broth, soy sauce, dark brown sugar, sesame oil, and garlic. Set the pressure cooker to heat or sauté mode.

Heat oil in the cooker, when hot, brown beef slices lightly on both sides. Pour the sauce over the beef, tossing the strips to coat.

Close and lock the lid and set the timer for 20 minutes. Release the pressure manually and carefully remove the lid. Seal the pressure valve.

Take 4 Tbsp. of the sauce and whisk it in a small bowl with the corn starch.

Set the pressure cooker on the heat or sauté mode.

Stir mixture slowly into the pressure cooker, add the broccoli and stir and simmer for 5-10 minutes until the broccoli is cooked and the sauce is thickened.

Great served over cooked rice.

Irish Stew

Servings: 6

Ingredients:

- 1 1/2 lbs. stew meat
- 1/4 cup extra virgin olive oil
- 1 (10 1/4 ounce) can tomato soup
- 1 (14 ounce) can chicken broth (or water)
- 4 carrots, coarsely chopped
- 4 large potatoes, peeled and cut into chunks
- 4 stalks celery, coarsely chopped
- 4 onions (half coarsely chopped, half diced)
- 2 teaspoons kosher salt
- 1 teaspoon fresh ground pepper
- 1/3 cup fresh parsley (chopped fine)
- 1 (12 ounce) can beer
- 2 bay leaves

Directions:

Pre-heat pressure cooker on heat or sauté mode. Add oil and sear the meat on all sides.

Remove meat from the pressure cooker and set aside. Pour beer or ale or water into hot pc and deglaze the pot.

Return the meat and the rest of the ingredients into the pressure cooker and mix well. Close and lock lid and make sure the pressure valve is sealed.

Set the timer for 25 minutes and when done release pressure manually. Open the lid and let sit for 5 minutes, then serve.

Greek Baby Back Ribs

Ingredients

- 2-3 lbs. slab of pork baby back ribs
- 4 cup apple juice
- 2 tablespoon *Greek seasoning*
- 2 tablespoon liquid smoke
- 2 dried minced onion
- 2 tablespoon cornstarch
- 2 tablespoons cold water

Instructions

Cut ribs into 3-4 ribs sections, place aside

Mix together apple juice, Greek seasoning, liquid smoke and dried minced onion in the cooker

Place ribs in mixture, cover and set the timer for 30 minutes. Seal the pressure valve.

When the pressure cooking time is up, release the pressure naturally. Open the lid and remove the ribs.

Whisk together the cornstarch and water to a smooth slurry and pour into the cooking liquid.

Stir constantly until liquid thickens into a gravy. Pour gravy over the ribs and serve.

Slow Cooker Braised Steak

Ingredients

- 1 lb blade steak (also called "minute" or "chicken" steak)
- 1 can (10.75 oz) cream of mushroom soup*
- 1 envelope Au Jus gravy mix
- 1 tbs. dehydrated (instant) onion flakes
- 1 small bay leaf
- 1/2 cup water
- 2 tbs. olive oil
- 1 bay leaf

Directions

Mix the soup, au jus mix and dehydrated onion in a small bowl. Add bay leaf. Heat oil in the pressure cooker in the heat setting.

Brown steaks in the oil on each side. Remove the steaks from the pressure cooker.

Deglaze the cooker with the 1/2 cup of water, scraping up all the browned bits in the cooker pan

Add the steaks back into the pressure cooker and pour the soup mixture over them. Cover and lock lid.

Seal the pressure valve and set the timer for 15 minutes. When the cooking time is up do a quick release.

Remove the steaks to a serving platter. Stir the gravy in the pressure cooker and remove bay leaf.

Pour the gravy over the steaks.

Serves 2

Sweet Pepper Steak

Ingredients

- 1½ - 2lbs steak, sliced very thin (I used sirloin for this recipe)
- 1 medium onion, sliced thin
- 1 red pepper, sliced
- ¾ cup soy sauce
- 1 cup water
- 1 tbsp garlic
- ½ tsp ground ginger
- ½ cup hoisin sauce
- ½ cup apricot jam
- 3 tbsp corn starch
- 3 tbsp water
- 2 tablespoons of olive oil

Instructions

Heat the oil to the pressure cooker in the heat mode

Place the steak pieces in the pressure cooker. Brown the steak pieces on both sides

Add the peppers and onions and stir to sauté

Combine the soy sauce, water, garlic, ginger, hoisin sauce, and apricot jam in a medium bowl. Pour into the pressure cooker. Set the timer for 15 minutes. Seal the pressure valve.

When the pressure cooking time is up release the pressure manually.

Combine the corn starch and water till smooth. Stir into sauce in the pressure cooker to thicken. Serve over noodles or rice.

Alaskan Amber PC Roast

Ingredients

- 3 pound tri-tip roast.
- 4-6 large red potatoes, quartered
- 1 large onion, chopped
- 3 cloves garlic, chopped
- 12 ounces Alaskan Amber of any amber ale
- Salt

Directions

Place the onions and garlic in the bottom of the pressure cooker. Pour in the Alaskan Amber and add the meat. Close the lid and set the timer for 45 minutes. Seal the pressure valve.

Release the pressure naturally (unplug). When the pressure is released, open the lid and remove the roast to a cutting board.

Add the potatoes to the pressure cooker, plug in, close the lid and set the timer for 6 minutes.

When done quick release the pressure, open the lid and remove the potatoes.

Slice the roast and serve with the potatoes.

Pressure Cooker Pepper Steak

Yield: 6

Ingredients

- 2 tablespoons vegetable oil
- 1 (2 1/2 pound) beef sirloin, cut into strips
- 1 teaspoon salt
- 1 1/2 cups beef broth
- 1 tablespoon cornstarch
- 2 medium onions, sliced
- 2 peppers, chopped
- 3 cloves garlic, chopped
- 1 (18 oz) can Progresso Fire Roasted Tomato Recipe Starter Cooking Sauce
- 3 tablespoons soy sauce
- 1 tablespoon honey
- 3 cups cooked rice

Directions

Set the pressure cooker to the heat or sauté mode. Add oil till hot.

Season beef with salt then add to pc pan and cook until browned (4-5 minutes)

Add beef broth to a mixing bowl then whisk in cornstarch. Pour mixture over beef in the pressure cooker.

Scatter onions, peppers and garlic over beef then add Fire Roasted Tomato Recipe Starter, soy sauce and honey.

Close and lock the lid, seal the pressure valve and then set the timer for 15 minutes.

When the cooking time is done release the pressure on its own (naturally). Open the lid.

Serve beef, onions and peppers with cooked rice.

Pressure Cooker Mongolian Beef

Serves: 2-4

Ingredients

- 1 ½ pounds Flank Steak
- ¼ cups cornstarch
- 2 tablespoons Olive Oil
- ½ teaspoons mince Garlic, Cloves
- ¾ cups Soy Sauce
- ¾ cups Water
- ¾ cups Brown Sugar
- 1 cup grated Carrots
- green onions, for garnish

Instructions

Cut flank steak into thin strips. In a zip lock bag add flank steak pieces and cornstarch. Shake to coat.

Add olive oil, minced garlic, soy sauce, water, brown sugar and carrots to pressure cooker. Stir ingredients. Add coated flank steak and stir again until coated in the sauce.

Close and lock the lid and set the timer for 20 minutes. Release the pressure naturally,

You can over rice and garnish with green onions.

Pressure Cooker-Teriyaki Pork Recipe

Serves 8

Ingredients

- 2 – 12 ounce pork tenderloins
- 1/2 cup reduced sodium soy sauce
- 1/4 cup rice vinegar
- 3 tablespoons brown sugar, packed
- 2 tablespoons vegetable oil
- 2 teaspoons fresh ginger, grated
- 2 cloves garlic, minced
- 1/2 teaspoon pepper
- 1 recipe Asian Coleslaw (link below)
- sesame seeds (optional)

Directions

Add a trivet to the pressure cooker. In a small bowl whisk together soy sauce, vinegar, brown sugar, oil, ginger, garlic and pepper.

Make a slice in the pork every few inches. Place pork on the trivet. Pour the soy sauce over the meat.

Cover and set the timer for 40 minutes. Seal the pressure valve.

When the cooking time is up let the pressure release naturally.

Transfer meat to a cutting board, reserving cooking liquid; cut meat into 1/2-inch slices. Serve with Asian Coleslaw. Drizzle meat with cooking liquid. Sprinkle with sesame seeds.

Pressure Cooker Cranberry Pork Roast

Serves 4

Ingredients

- 2-3 pounds pork loin roast
- Salt and pepper
- 2 tablespoons olive oil
- 1 medium white onion, chopped
- 1 cup dried cranberries
- 1/4 cup Cascadian Farm™ organic blackberry fruit spread
- 1 teaspoon chili powder
- 1 bay leaf
- 1 cup vegetable stock
- 1 cup water

Directions

Season pork roast with salt and pepper on all sides. Heat the oil in the pressure cooker set on heat or sauté.

Once the oil is hot, add pork roast and sear for 2-3 minutes on all sides. Add the onions and cook for about 3 minutes.

Pour water into the pan and scrape up any bits in the pan. Add the cranberries, blackberry spread, chili powder, vegetable stock and bay leaf.

Close and lock the lid and seal the pressure valve. Set the timer for 35 minutes. When the cooking time is up allow the pressure to release naturally.

Test pork temperature with a meat thermometer. It should register 145-150°F in the thickest part of the roast. Remove meat to a serving tray and thicken sauce, if desired, by continuing to cook for a few minutes more in the heat or sauté mode (or by mixing a teaspoon of corn starch with a teaspoon of water until smooth and whisking it into the sauce).

Slice roast into 1/4-inch or 1/2-inch slices. Serve the pork drizzled with sauce from the pressure cooker.

Bloody Mary Steak

Ingredients

- 1 1/2 lbs. skirt steak
- 1 cup spicy Bloody Mary mix
- 2 oz. vodka
- 1 lemon, sliced and juiced

Directions

Add steak to a large plastic bag. In a bowl, stir together Bloody Mary mix, vodka and lemon juice.

Pour marinade into the bag over steak and add sliced lemons. Marinate for at least an hour, but overnight is best.

Remove steak from marinade and brown in oil in the cooker set on the heat mode for 5-6 minutes per side.

Pour the marinade over the browned steak. Close and lock the lid and set the timer for 20 minutes.

Seal the pressure valve. When the cooking cycle is done reduce the pressure manually and open the lid.

Remove and then slice or chop steak and serve while warm.

Cider Beef Pot Roast with Sweet Potatoes

Serves 4-6

Ingredients

- 1 beef shoulder roast or beef chuck pot roast, boneless (2.5 to 3.5 pounds)
- 2 to 4 tablespoons olive oil
- 1 teaspoon salt
- 1/2 teaspoon pepper
- 1 large white onion, chopped
- 2 teaspoons thyme crushed thyme leaves
- 2 cups ready-to-serve beef broth
- 1 1/2 cup apple cider
- 1 1/2 pound sweet potatoes, peeled, cut crosswise into 1- to 1-1/2-inch pieces
- 5 cloves garlic, chopped finely
- 1 tablespoon maple syrup
- 1/3 cup chunky applesauce
- 2 to 3 tablespoons cornstarch, dissolved in 2 to 3 tablespoons of water

Instructions

Set the pressure cooker in the heat mode and add olive oil.

Pat raw beef with a paper towel and rub with salt and pepper mixture.

Place the beef in the pressure cooker and cook the beef until brown on both sides.

Remove to a plate. Add the onion and place in the bottom of the pressure cooker.

Sprinkle chopped garlic over the onions. Place sweet potatoes over onion and garlic.

In a large bowl, combine thyme, beef broth, apple cider, applesauce, and maple syrup. Stir thoroughly.

Place browned beef over onion, garlic, and sweet potatoes in the pressure cooker. Pour the sauce mixture over the beef, potatoes, onion and garlic.

Close and lock the lid and set the timer for 60 minutes. Seal the pressure valve.

When the cooking time is done release the pressure naturally and open the lid. Remove the roast from the cooker and set aside.

If needed, pour in cornstarch mixture and stir the liquid gravy in the cooker.

Return the roast to the pressure cooker. Continue cooking the roast uncovered for another 10 minutes, until desired gravy thickness is reached.

When roast is done cooking, slice and serve. Pour gravy on top for serving.

Serve with sweet potatoes from the cooker.

Ranch Pressure Pork Chops

Serves 4

Ingredients

- 4 pork chops, about 1/2" thick
- 1 tablespoon oil for browning
- 1 Tbsp. ranch dressing mix from a store bought packet)
- 1 10-oz can cream of chicken soup
- ¼ cup of water
- Cooked Mashed Potatoes

Direction

Set the pressure cooker the the heat or saute mode and add the oil.

Quickly brown the pork chops on both sides in the cooker in the hot oil, giving them a quick sear.

Sprinkle with the ranch dressing mix. Pour the chicken soup mixed with the water over the top.

Close and lock the lid and set the timer for 10 minutes. Seal the pressure valve.

When the time is up let the pressure release naturally. Remove the pork chops, serve with mashed potatoes and sauce.

Pressure Cooked Spaghetti & Meat sauce

Serves 4

Ingredients

- 2 tablespoons olive oil
- 1 pound ground beef
- 1 cup chopped onion
- 1 clove garlic, mashed
- 2 cans (8 oz. size) tomato sauce
- 2 cups dry red wine
- 1 cup water
- 1 lb. spaghetti pasta, uncooked
- 1 1/2 teaspoon chili powder
- 1 1/2 teaspoon salt
- 1/4 cup grated Parmesan cheese

Directions

Set the pressure cooker to heat and add oil. When the oil is hot add the beef, onion and garlic.

Stirring occasionally to sauté onions and separate the beef. Stir until the beef is browned.

Add all remaining ingredients except cheese. Toss uncooked pasta in liquid so it separates

(if spaghetti is to long break strands in half before adding)..

Close and lock the lid. Seal the pressure valve. Set the timer for 8 minutes

When the cooking time is up release the pressure manually. Open the lid and stir in cheese.

Veal Chop PC

Serves 4

Ingredients

- 1 (4-5-pound) boned and rolled veal shoulder or rump (save bones for veal stock)
- 2 tablespoons cooking oil
- 2 large yellow onions, peeled and coarsely chopped
- 1-2 cloves garlic, peeled and crushed
- 1 carrot, peeled and chopped fine
- 1 stalk celery, chopped fine
- 1 bay leaf and 1 sprig each parsley and thyme, tied in cheesecloth (bouquet garni)
- 2 teaspoons salt
- 1/4 teaspoon pepper
- 1/3 cup cold water
- 1/4 cup unsifted flour
- 3 cups veal stock or a 1/2 and 1/2 mixture of beef and chicken broths
- 1-2 teaspoons liquid gravy browner (optional)

Directions

Set the pressure cooker to brown or sauté and add the oil. Brown all sides of veal and the onion in oil in the open pressure cooker.

Add garlic, carrot, celery, bay leaf, parsley, thyme, salt, pepper, and water. Close and lock the lid, set the timer for 35 minutes. Seal the pressure valve.

When the cooking cycle is complete, reduce pressure naturally, open cooker, remove veal and keep warm. Discard bouquet garni.

Puree vegetables and any remaining liquid by buzzing 20 to 30 seconds in an electric blender at low speed or 15 to 20 seconds in a food processor fitted with the metal chopping blade. Blend flour with 1 cup of stock. Add remaining stock and puree into cooker and bring to a boil.

Stir in flour paste and cook, stirring, until thickened. Let simmer 2 to 3 minutes. Taste for seasoning and adjust. Slice 1/4" thick pieces and top with gravy.

Pressure Cooker BBQ Ribs

Serves 4

Ingredients

- 3 lbs. spareribs, cut into serving pieces
- salt and pepper
- paprika
- 3 teaspoons vegetable oil
- 4 onions, sliced
- 2 cups ketchup
- 1 cup vinegar
- 2 teaspoons Worcestershire sauce
- 1 teaspoon chili powder
- 1 teaspoon celery seed

Directions

Season ribs with salt, pepper and paprika. Set the pressure cooker to heat and add the oil.

Brown ribs a few at a time on both sides, then remove.

Add onions and sauté for 3-5 minutes till softened. Combine remaining ingredients in a bowl,

Add back all the ribs and pour the combined ingredients over them.

Close and lock the lid and seal the pressure valve. Set the timer for 20 minutes.

When the time is up, release the pressure naturally.

Open the lid and carefully remove the ribs. Spoon sauce over the ribs and serve or put under a broiler to carmelize and the serve.

Fast, Rich Pressure-Cooker Beef Stock

Ingredients

- 2 tablespoons tomato paste
- 3 pounds meaty beef marrow bones
- 2 1/2 pounds (1-inch-thick) beef shanks
- 2 celery stalks, diagonally cut into 2-inch pieces
- 1 large carrot, peeled and diagonally cut into 2-inch pieces
- 1 large onion, peeled and cut into 8 wedges
- Cooking spray
- 1 tablespoon black peppercorns
- 2 bay leaves
- 1/2 bunch fresh flat-leaf parsley
- 8 cups cold water

Preparation

Preheat oven to 500°.

Brush tomato paste evenly over bones and shanks; place in a large roasting pan. Add celery, carrot, and onion to pan; lightly coat with cooking spray. Bake at 500° for 30 minutes.

Transfer bone mixture to a 6- or 8-quart pressure cooker; add pepper corns, bay leaves, and parsley. Pour 8 cups water over mixture. Close lid securely, and set the timer for 45 minutes.

Reduce the pressure naturally, remove lid, and let stand for 20 minutes. Strain stock through a cheesecloth-lined sieve into a large bowl, pressing solids to release excess moisture. Discard solids. Cover and chill overnight.

Skim solidified fat from surface; discard.

Note: Refrigerate stock for up to 1 week or freeze for up to 3 months.

Coconut Beef

Ingredients

- 1-2 lbs. stew meat
- 1 yellow onion, cut in chunks
- 1 can coconut milk
- 1 juice from one lime
- 2 Teaspoons of butter
- 2 cloves chopped garlic
- 2 tsp brown sugar
- 1 tsp curry powder
- 1/2 tsp ground coriander
- 1 tsp cumin
- 1 1/2 T chili paste (or 1-2 tsp red chili flakes)
- 1" piece of ginger, peeled and grated

Directions

Set the pressure cooker to the heat or sauté mode. Put the butter into the pressure cooker and heat till it melts.

Add the meat and brown on both sides for 5 minutes. When all the meat is browned add the lime juice, and coconut milk.

Follow with the onion and garlic. Add the brown sugar and all the spices. Grate in the ginger.

Toss meat a bit in the liquid and spices to coat.

Cover and lock the lid and set the timer for 25 minutes. Seal the pressure valve.

When the time is up, let the pressure reduce naturally. The coconut milk will be yellow from the curry, and will separate a bit.

Giving it a quick stir will make it all creamy again. Serve over white or brown rice.

Easy Fajita Beef

Ingredients

- 2 lbs. of thin cut stir fry beef
- 1 packets of fajita seasoning mix
- 1 onion
- 2 bell peppers (I used 1 orange, 1 yellow)
- 1/2 cup of water

Directions

Dump your meat into the pressure cooker. Add the onion and the peppers in strips.

Add the seasoning and water and mix. Cover, lock the lid and set the timer for 12 minutes.

Seal the pressure valve. When the pressure cooking time is up release the pressure naturally.

Serve with your favorite fajita fixings. Try squeezing some fresh lime over the top of the meat before doctoring it up.

Beer Braised Pork Roast

Serves 4

Ingredients

- 2 tablespoons Dark Brown Sugar
- 1 tbsp. smoked paprika
- 1 tbsp. ground black pepper
- 1 tbsp. dried oregano
- 1 tbsp. seasoned salt
- 3 lbs. pork butt roast
- 2 tbsp. olive oil
- 1 medium onion, cut into quarters, roots and skin removed
- 4 cloves of garlic, finely chopped
- 1 medium carrot, cut into big chunks
- 8 ounces sliced mushrooms
- 2 bottles (12 ounces) brown ale beer or other dark beer
- 1 can (4.5 ounces) low sodium beef broth
- 3 tablespoons cornstarch
- ¼ cup water

Instructions

Combine the brown sugar, paprika, black pepper, salt and oregano in a small bowl and set aside.

Rub the dry spice mixture over the pork pieces until they are well coated. Heat the oil in the pressure cooker in the heat, brown or sauté mode. Sear meat on each side. Stir in all of the ingredients close and lock the lid. Seal the pressure valve. Set the timer for 30 minutes.

When the cooking time is done reduce the pressure naturally.

Open the lid and remove the pork and vegetables. Set the cooker to heat or sauté and bring to a boil. While broth is coming to a boil, mix cornstarch with water till smooth. Pour into boiling mixture, stir till blended and thickened.

To serve spoon sauce over pork and vegetables.

Korean Beef

Serves 4-6

Ingredients

- 1 cup beef broth
- 3 lb. boneless beef chuck roast, cut into 1-inch cubes
- 1/2 cup reduced sodium soy sauce
- 1/2 cup brown sugar, packed
- 4 cloves garlic, minced
- 1 tablespoon sesame oil
- 1 tablespoon rice wine vinegar
- 1 tablespoon freshly grated ginger
- 1 teaspoon Sriracha, or more, to taste
- 1/2 teaspoon onion powder
- 1/2 teaspoon white pepper
- 2 tablespoons cornstarch
- 1 teaspoon sesame seeds
- 2 green onions, thinly sliced

Instructions

In a large bowl, whisk together beef broth, soy sauce, brown sugar, garlic, sesame oil, rice wine vinegar, ginger, Sriracha, onion powder and white pepper.

Place chuck roast into the pressure cooker. Stir in beef broth mixture until well combined. Cover and set the timer for 25 minutes. Seal the pressure valve.

Release the pressure naturally when done. Open the lid.

In a small bowl, whisk together corn starch and 1/4 cup water. Stir in mixture into the pressure cooker. Simmer in the heat mode for additional 10 minutes, or until the sauce has thickened.

Serve immediately, garnished with green onions and sesame seeds, if desired

Cashew Beef with Broccoli

Serves 2

Ingredients

- 1 lb. boneless, beef chuck roast, sliced into thin strips
- 1 cup beef broth
- ½ cup low sodium soy sauce
- ⅓ Cup dark brown sugar
- 1 tbsp. sesame oil
- 3 garlic cloves minced
- 2 tbsp. cornstarch
- 3 cups Frozen Broccoli Florets
- 1 cup cashews
- 1 cup frozen carrots
- White or brown rice, cooked

Directions

In a mixing bowl, whisk together the beef broth, soy sauce, dark brown sugar, sesame oil and garlic.

Lay the beef strips in the pressure cooker, add carrots and pour the sauce over, tossing the strips to coat.

Close and lock the lid, seal the pressure valve and set the timer for 15 minutes.

When the cooking cycle is done release the pressure manually. Open the lid. Set cooker to heat.

Take 4 tbsp. of the sauce from the pot and whisk it in a small bowl with the corn starch till smooth.

Slowly stir this into the pressure cooker. Add the broccoli and cashews and stir.

Simmer for an additional 5-10 minutes in the heat mode with the lid off.

Cook until the sauce can thicken and the broccoli is cooked. Serve over rice.

POULTRY

Chicken Cacciatore

Ingredients

- 3 tbs. olive oil
- 2 lbs. boneless chicken breast, cut into 2 inch cubes
- ¼ cups chicken broth
- 1 cup white cooking wine
- 14 oz. sliced mushrooms
- 1 large onion minced
- 2 tsp. garlic powder or 1 crushed clove
- 1 small bunch fresh basil
- 1 small can tomato paste
- ½ teaspoon thyme

Procedure

Set the pressure cooker to heat or sauté and add the oil.

Add the chicken and cook and stir for 5 minutes or until brown on all sides

Add the onions and sauté till softened. Add the broth, wine, garlic, tomato paste and mushrooms.

Toss in the basil and thyme.

Close and lock lid. Set the timer for 10 minutes.

When the cooking time is up release the pressure manually. Remove the lid.

Serve over cooked pasta or rice.

Chicken Fricassee

....

Ingredients

- 1 chicken, cut into serving pieces
- 3 carrots, cut into 1 inch pieces
- Small piece of salt pork diced
- 2 celery stalks, cut into 1 inch pieces
- 1-1/2 tsp. olive oil
- 1 onion, cut into wedges
- 1 cup chicken stock
- 1 tsp. dried marjoram
- 1 Tbs. fresh chives or parsley, minced
- garlic clove

Procedure

Set the pressure cooker to heat or sauté and add the oil.

Season chicken and add to cooker, turning until brown on all sides.

Add the onion, garlic, carrots and celery and sauté with the chicken for 3-5 minutes

Stir in stock and marjoram. Close and lock the lid and seal the pressure valve.

Set the timer for 20 minutes at high pressure.

When the cooking time is up release the pressure manually. Open the lid and serve.

Chicken Liver Pate

Ingredients

- 3/4 lb chicken livers
- 1 medium onion, chopped
- 1 bay leaf
- 1/2 of a cup of red wine, rum or whiskey
- 2 anchovies in oil
- 1 Tbs capers
- 1 Tbs butter
- Salt & pepper

Procedure

Set the pressure cooker to heat or sauté with the lid off. Add the oil.

Add the onions and salt and pepper and cook onions till translucent

Add the chicken and bay leaf and cook for 2 minutes, stirring.

Add wine and with wooden spoon loosen any brown bits stuck to the pot

Close and lock the lid and seal the pressure valve. Set the timer for 3 minutes

When the cooking time is up release the pressure manually and open the lid.

Remove the bay leaf. Add anchovies, butter and capers and blend with an immersion blender

Mix well and place in serving dish garnished with herbs.

Chicken Pilaf

Ingredients

- 2 tbs. oil
- 4 chicken breasts, boneless, skinless (cut into bite sized pieces)
- 1 onion, chopped
- 1 cup uncooked long-grain rice
- 2 cups vegetables (peas, carrots, corn) frozen or fresh.
- 2 ½ cups of chicken broth
- 1 tsp curry powder
- 1/2 tsp ground cinnamon
- 1 bay leaf

Procedure

Set the pressure cooker to the heat mode and add the oil..

Place chicken in the pressure cooker and brown in batches.

Remove the browned chicken and cover to keep warm.

Add onions and sauté about 3 minutes until translucent.

Add rice and stir to slightly brown.

Add the broth, vegetables, curry powder, cinnamon and bay leaf and stir.

Add the chicken back to the cooker. Close and lock lid and seal the pressure valve.

Set the timer for 8 minutes. When the cooking time is up wait 5 minutes then release the pressure.

Remove the bay leaf and fluff. Serve warm.

Cranberry Turkey Wings

Ingredients

- 2 tbs. butter
- 2 tbs. oil
- 4 turkey wings
- Salt and pepper
- Small bundle of thyme
- 1 cup dry cranberries (soaked in boiling water for 5 minutes) or
- 1 1/2 cup fresh cranberries or
- 1 cup of canned cranberries, rinsed
- 1 medium onion sliced
- 1 cup shelled walnuts
- 1 cup orange juice

Procedure

Set the pressure cooker to the heat or saute mode and add the butter

Add the turkey wings and brown wings on all sides

Add salt and pepper

Remove wings and add onions to cooker and cook till translucent

Place wings on onions

Add cranberries, walnuts, small bundle of thyme

Pour orange juice over the turkey. Close and lock the lid and seal the pressure valve.

Set the timer for 8 minutes. When the cooking time is up release the pressure manually.

Open the lid and remove the thyme.

Place wings on an oven proof serving tray

Place tray in oven and broil for 5 minutes to caramelize

Pour contents of cooker over wings and serve

Creamy Chicken Tortilla Casserole

Serves 2-4

Ingredients

- 2 diced chicken breasts
- 1/2 can cream of chicken soup
- 1 cup chunky salsa
- 3/4 cup grated cheddar cheese divided (1/2 cup and 1/4 cup)
- 1 4 oz. can diced green chilies
- 1 teaspoon ground cumin
- 1 tablespoon adobo sauce
- 4 flour tortillas

Procedure

Butter a 7x3 baking dish.

Mix the chicken, soup, salsa, chilies, cumin and adobo sauce and ½ cup of cheese.

Place a flower tortilla in the pan and add the chicken mixture on top.

Repeat using the remaining tortillas and chicken mixture ending with tortilla.

Top with the ¼ cup remaining cheese.

Butter a piece of foil and use it to securely cover the baking dish.

Place a trivet and 1 cup water in the pressure cooker and place the covered dish on top.

Close and lock the lid and seal the pressure valve. Set the timer for 10 minutes.

When the pressure cooking time is up release the pressure manually.

Remove the foil and serve with extra salsa

Herbed Chicken and Mushrooms

Ingredients

- 3 lbs. chicken thighs and/or drumsticks, skinned
- 1 tablespoon oil
- 5 cups sliced assorted fresh mushrooms, such as shiitake, button, crimini, and/or oyster
- 1 red onion, cut into wedges
- 1/2 cup chopped carrot (1 medium)
- 1/4 cup dried tomato pieces (not oil-packed)
- 3/4 cup chicken broth
- 1/4 cup dry white wine or chicken broth
- 3 tablespoons quick-cooking tapioca, crushed
- 1 teaspoon dried thyme, crushed
- 1/2 teaspoon garlic salt
- 1/2 teaspoon dried basil, crushed
- 1/4 teaspoon ground black pepper
- 4 1/2 cups hot cooked plain and/or spinach linguine or fettuccine, or hot cooked rice.

Procedure

Add oil to heated pressure cooker. Brown the chicken in batches in the oil for about 5 minutes.

Remove the chicken from the pot and add the remaining ingredients (except the pasta or rice).

Close the lid and set the timer for 12 minutes. Seal the pressure.

When the cooking time is up release the pressure manually.

Serve over rice or pasta.

Cowboy Casserole

Ingredients

- 1 onion, chopped
- 1 1/2 lbs. ground chuck, browned and drained (in pressure cooker)
- 6 medium potatoes, sliced
- 1 can red beans
- 1 (8 ounce) can tomatoes mixed with 2 tablespoons flour or 1 can tomato soup
- Salt and pepper and garlic to taste
- 1 cup water

Procedure

Put oil and chopped onion in the bottom of the pressure cooker; mix in the beef and brown on heat mode.

Add the sliced potatoes and beans and the tomatoes or tomato soup on top of the beef, then add the water.

Sprinkle with seasonings as desired. Cover and set timer for 15 minutes.

Seal the pressure valve. When time is up release the pressure manually.

If needed simmer sauce in the cooker till thickened. Serve hot.

Chicken & Shrimp Jambalaya

Ingredients

- 1 pound skinless, boneless chicken breast halves or thighs
- 2 cups thinly sliced celery (4 stalks)
- 2 cups chopped onion (2 large)
- 1 14 1/2 ounce can no-salt-added diced tomatoes, undrained
- 1 14 ounce can reduced-sodium chicken broth
- 1/2 6 ounce can no-salt-added tomato paste (1/3 cup)
- 1 1/2 teaspoons salt-free Cajun seasoning
- 2 cloves garlic, minced
- 1/2 teaspoon salt
- 1 1/2 cups uncooked instant brown rice
- 3/4 cup chopped green, red, and/or yellow sweet pepper
- 8 ounces peeled and deveined cooked shrimp*
- 2 tablespoons snipped fresh Italian (flat-leaf) parsley
- Celery leaves (optional)

Procedure

Add all ingredients to pressure cooker except the shrimp. Mix, close and lock the lid.

Set timer for 12 minutes. When the cooking time is up, release the pressure manually.

Open the lid and dump in the shrimp, stir and warm for 3-5 minutes and serve.

Serves 4 to 6.

Garlic Chicken with Artichokes

Ingredients

- 2 medium red sweet peppers, cut into 1-inch-wide strips
- 2 medium onions, cut in wedges
- 12 cloves garlic, peeled
- 1 tablespoon quick-cooking tapioca
- 2 teaspoons dried rosemary, crushed
- 1 teaspoon finely shredded lemon peel
- 1/2 teaspoon ground black pepper
- 1/2 cup chicken broth
- 3 pounds skinless, boneless chicken thighs
- 1 8 oz. package frozen artichoke hearts
- 1 tablespoon lemon juice
- 4 cups hot cooked brown rice

Procedure

In the pressure cooker combine sweet peppers, onions, garlic, tapioca, rosemary, lemon peel, and black pepper.

Pour broth over the mixture in pressure cooker. Add the chicken.

Cover and set the timer for 8 minutes. Release pressure manually and open lid.

Stir in frozen artichoke hearts and lemon juice.

Cook on heat uncovered for about 10 minutes more or until the artichokes are done. Serve with rice.

Pressure Cooker Coq au Vin

Ingredients

- 1 tablespoon Olive oil
- 3 lbs. chicken thighs, skinned
- 1 envelope (1/2 of a 2.2-ounce package) beefy onion soup mix
- 2 cups quartered fresh mushrooms
- 1 1/2 cups frozen small whole onions
- 3 medium carrots, cut into 31/2-inch sticks
- 1/2 cup dry red wine
- Hot cooked mashed potatoes (optional)
- Snipped fresh parsley (optional)

Procedure

Set the pressure cooker to heat. Add the oil till hot. Cook chicken thighs, several at a time, in the pressure cooker until brown. Drain off fat.

Sprinkle with dry soup mix. Add mushrooms, onions, and carrots. Pour wine over all.

Cover and lock the lid and set the timer for 12 minutes. Seal the pressure valve. When the cooking time is up release the pressure manually. If desired, serve with mashed potatoes sprinkled with parsley.

Cacciatore-Style Chicken

Ingredients

- 2 cups sliced fresh mushrooms
- 1 cup sliced celery
- 1 cup chopped carrot
- 2 medium onions, cut into wedges
- 1 yellow, green, or red sweet pepper, cut into strips
- 4 cloves garlic, minced
- 12 chicken drumsticks, skinned (about 3-1/2 lbs. total)
- 1/2 cup chicken broth
- 1/4 cup dry white wine
- 2 tablespoons quick-cooking tapioca
- 2 bay leaves
- 1 teaspoon dried oregano, crushed
- 1 teaspoon sugar
- 1/2 teaspoon salt
- 1/4 teaspoon ground black pepper
- 1 14 1/2 ounce can diced tomatoes, undrained
- 1/3 cup tomato paste
- Hot cooked pasta or rice
- Shredded basil (optional)

Procedure

Combine mushrooms, celery, carrot, onions, sweet pepper, and garlic in the pressure cooker.

Place chicken drumsticks on vegetables. Add broth, wine, tapioca, bay leaves, oregano, sugar, salt, and pepper.

Cover set the timer for 10 minutes. When the cooking time is done release the pressure manually.

Remove chicken and keep warm. Discard bay leaves. Set cooker to heat or sauté. Stir in undrained tomatoes and tomato paste. Cook uncovered for 5 minutes more. To serve, spoon vegetable mixture over chicken and pasta. If desired, garnish with basil. Makes 6 servings.

Kickin' Chicken Chili

Ingredients

- 2 pounds skinless, boneless chicken breast halves or thighs, cut into 1-inch pieces
- 2 teaspoons ground cumin
- 1/4 teaspoon salt
- 1 tablespoon olive oil or cooking oil
- 1 16 ounce jar green salsa
- 1 16 oz. package frozen pepper stir-fry vegetables (yellow, green, and red sweet peppers, and onion)
- 1 15 oz. can cannellini beans (white kidney beans), rinsed and drained
- 1 14 1/2 oz. can of diced tomatoes with onion and garlic
- Dairy sour cream (optional)
- Shredded cheese (optional)

Procedure

In a large bowl, toss chicken with cumin and salt to coat. Set the pressure cooker to the heat or sauté mode. Cook the chicken, half at a time till browned on all sides. Drain off the fat. Stir in salsa, stir-fry vegetables, beans, and undrained tomatoes.

Cover and lock the lid and seal the pressure valve. Set the timer for 10 minutes. When the cooking time is up release the pressure manually.

If desired, top with sour cream and cheese. Makes 4 (1-1/2-cup) servings and reserves.

Saucy Sweet and Sour Chicken

Ingredients

- 2 1/2 pounds meaty chicken pieces (breast halves, thighs, and drumsticks), skinned
- 1/4 teaspoon salt
- 1/2 12 ounce can (about 3/4 cup) frozen lemonade concentrate, thawed
- 1/4 cup water
- 3 tablespoons brown sugar
- 3 tablespoons ketchup
- 1 tablespoon vinegar
- 2 tablespoons cornstarch
- 2 tablespoons cold water
- Hot cooked rice or fried rice

Procedure

Place chicken pieces in the pressure cooker. Sprinkle with salt. In a medium bowl, combine lemonade concentrate, water, brown sugar, ketchup, and vinegar. Pour over chicken in cooker.

Cover and set timer for 10 minutes. When the cooking time is up release the pressure manually and transfer chicken to a serving platter; cover and keep warm.

Skim off the fat from the cooking liquid in the pressure cooker. For sauce, combine cornstarch and the cold water; stir into liquid in pressure cooker. Stir uncovered in the heat or sauté mode until thickened and bubbly. Cook and stir for 2 minutes more. Spoon sauce over chicken.

Chicken Pot Pie

Serves 4

Ingredients

- (1) 10 3/4 ounce can Cream of Chicken Soup
- (1) 10 3/4 ounce can Cream of Celery Soup
- (1) 10 3/4 ounce can Cream of Onion Soup
- (1) 10 3/4 ounce can Chicken Broth (near cream soups)
- 1 Pound Boneless Skinless Chicken Breasts, cut into 1 inch cubes
- 1/2 cup white onions, diced
- 1 cup carrots, sliced
- 2 medium sized baking potatoes, peeled and cubed
- 1/2 teaspoon dried thyme
- 1/2 teaspoon dried oregano
- 2 dashes of black pepper
- 1 cup frozen peas (add at end)

For Serving

- 1 Can Biscuits, baked in oven as per package directions

Instructions

In a big bowl mix together the soups, and chicken broth, whisk together until smooth, Add onions, carrots, potatoes, thyme, oregano, and black pepper to the pressure cooker. Add the chicken and stir.

Close and lock the lid and set the timer for 10 minutes. When the cooking time is up do a quick release and open

Add frozen peas, and stir. Set cooker to simmer until ready to serve. Cut the baked biscuits in half.

Serve the chicken pot pie filling over the baked biscuits.

General Taos Chicken

Serves 4-6

Ingredients:

- 4 boneless skinless chicken breasts
- 1/2 cup water
- 3 T hoisin sauce
- 2 T soy sauce
- 1/2 cup brown sugar
- 3 T ketchup
- 1/4 tsp dry ginger
- 1/2 tsp crushed red pepper (more or less to liking)
- 1 T cornstarch

Instructions

In a mixing bowl, mix together water, hoisin sauce, soy sauce, brown sugar, ketchup, ginger and crushed red pepper.

Place the chicken in the pressure cooker and then pour the sauce mixture over the chicken. Cover the pressure cooker and lock the lid.

Set the timer for 8 minutes. Seal the pressure valve.

When the pressure cooking time is up release the pressure manually.

Open the lid. Whisk cornstarch in the sauce to thicken it up.

Add chicken back to the pressure cooker and allow to simmer another 3 minutes. Serve over hot rice and garnish with toasted sesame seeds if desired.

Pressure Cooker Cranberry Glazed Chicken

Serves 4

Ingredients

- 4 chicken breasts
- 1 small yellow onion, diced
- 1 (14 ounce) can cranberry sauce
- 1 cup barbecue sauce
- 1 teaspoon salt
- ½ teaspoon dried thyme
- ¼ teaspoon ground ginger
- ¼ teaspoon black pepper
- instant mashed potatoes

Directions

Place the chicken and onion in the pressure cooker. Add all the remaining ingredients in a mixing bowl and stir to combine. Pour the sauce over the chicken.

Close and lock the lid and set the timer for 10 minutes. Seal the pressure valve.

When time is up wait 5 minutes and then release the pressure manually.

Serve with instant mashed potatoes with some extra sauce on the side.

Chicken and Spinach Curry

A different twist on a very healthy curry flavored dish with spinach and organic pasta sauce adding to the curry flavor.

Ingredients:

- **Step 1:** 2 lb boneless chicken breasts, skinned and chopped into 1" chunks.
- **Step 2:** 2 (10 oz each) packages frozen spinach, thawed
- **Step 3:** 2 tbsp. organic sugar free apple sauce
- ½ cup chicken broth
- 1 tbsp. mild curry powder
- 1 ½ cups organic sugar free pasta sauce
- Salt and freshly ground black pepper to taste
- Chopped fresh cilantro, for garnishing

Directions:

Set cooker to heat or sauté, add Olive Oil to the pressure cooker and brown chicken lightly.

Leave the chicken pieces in the pressure cooker and pour in the broth. Scatter the spinach leaves on top.

Whisk the curry powder into the pasta sauce until well mixed and drizzle it over the spinach.

Don't stir and secure the lid. Seal the pressure valve. Set the timer for 6 minutes.

When the cooking time is up release the pressure using the quick release method and unlock the cooker.

Spoon in the applesauce and stir all together to mix well.

Simmer the sauce, uncovered, for 5 minutes or until the sauce thickens slightly and adjust the seasonings.

Sprinkle the chopped cilantro over each serving and serve warm.

Serve with sautéed vegetables. **Serves:** 6

Mushroom Chicken

A combination of shiitake, button, crimini, and oyster. Make sure clean the mushrooms well.

Ingredients

- 3 pounds chicken thighs or drumsticks (with bone), skinned
- 5 cups sliced mixed fresh mushrooms
- 1 medium onion, chopped
- ½ cup chopped carrot
- 1/4 cup dried tomato pieces
- 3/4 cup chicken broth
- 1/4 cup dry white wine or water
- 3 tablespoons quick-cooking tapioca
- 1 teaspoon dried thyme, crushed
- ½ teaspoon dried basil, crushed
- ½ teaspoon garlic salt
- ½ teaspoon pepper
- 4 cups cooked spinach

Directions:

Place the mushrooms, onion, carrot, dried tomato, chicken broth, wine, tapioca, thyme, basil, garlic salt, and pepper into the pressure cooker and then top with the chicken.

Cover the cooker and set timer for 10 minutes. Seal the pressure valve.

When the cooking time is release the pressure manually

Serve the chicken over the spinach. Serves 4

Chicken Korma

Serves 4

Ingredients

- 4 boneless skinless chicken breasts, cut into bite-sized pieces, seasoned with salt and pepper
- 2 cups chopped onion
- 2 tablespoons peeled minced fresh ginger
- 1 teaspoon whole coriander seeds
- 2 teaspoons curry powder
- 1 teaspoon ground coriander
- 1/2 teaspoon cumin
- 1/2 teaspoon crushed red pepper flakes
- 8 garlic cloves, minced
- 2 cups peeled diced potatoes (about 4 large potatoes)
- 1 teaspoon salt
- 1 (14.5 oz.) can of diced tomatoes, undrained
- 2 bay leaves
- 1 3-inch cinnamon stick
- 1/2 cup whole milk plain yogurt
- 4 cups long-grain brown rice, cooked
- 1/4 cup chopped cilantro, for garnish
- Olive or coconut oil.

Directions

Set pressure cooker on sauté setting, and heat about 1 tablespoon of oil until hot. Brown chicken in batches until golden. Remove and set aside.

Add onions and whole coriander, and sauté until onions are translucent. Add remaining ingredients, except yogurt, rice, and cilantro.

Cover and set pressure cooker timer for 15 minutes. Seal the pressure valve.

Allow pressure to come down on its own naturally when the cooking time is done.

When ready to serve, stir in yogurt. Serve over rice, and garnish with cilantro.

SEAFOOD

Shrimp in Herbs

Ingredients

- 2 Tbs olive oil
- 1 ½ lbs large shrimp shelled and de-veined
- 1 cup minced onion
- 2 Tbs minced parsley
- 4 cloves garlic minced
- 2 tsp paprika
- ¼ cup dry white wine
- ½ cup fish stock or clam juice
- 1 cup tomato sauce
- Pinch of sugar
- Pinch of saffron
- 1 tsp crushed red pepper
- 1 bay leaf
- ¼ tsp thyme
- Salt, freshly ground pepper to taste

Procedure

Set the pressure cooker to heat or sauté, add the oil and sauté the shrimp lightly.

Remove shrimp to plate

Add onion and sauté until softened.

Stir in parsley, garlic, paprika and wine. Cook until wine is reduced by ½.

Add fish stock, tomato sauce, sugar, saffron, red pepper, bay leaf, thyme, salt and pepper.

Close and lock lid. Seal the pressure valve. Set the timer for 5 minutes. Seal the pressure valve.

When the cooking time is up release the pressure manually. Open the lid.

Set the cooker to heat or sauté, add the shrimp and simmer for a few minutes until the shrimp are fully cooked.

Remove bay leaf. Serve over rice.

Pressure Cooker Maple Salmon

Ingredients:

- 4 Salmon fillets
- 4 10" x 12" aluminum foil
- 1/2 cup maple syrup
- 1/8 cup lime juice
- 1/4 cup soy sauce
- 2 tsp crushed garlic
- 1 tsp minced ginger root
- 1 cup water

Directions:

In a mixing bowl mix together the maple syrup, lime juice, soy sauce and garlic.

Place each salmon filet on the center of a piece of foil and spoon on the mixture until completely covered.

Fold foil around the salmon to form a sealed packet.

Make sure the ends are sealed tightly.

Add the water to the pressure cooker and add a rack or trivet. Place the packets on the rack and close and lock the lid.

Seal the pressure valve. Set the timer as follows:

- 5 minutes for rare
- 6 minute for medium
- 8 minutes for cooked through.

If you are not sure, cook for 6 minute. When cooking time is up release the pressure manually.

Remove and check doneness.

If necessary, put back in cooker and set the timer for an additional 3-5 minutes then release the pressure. Serves 4

Salmon Garlic Cilantro

Ingredients

- 1 lb. salmon fillet (3 to 4 fillets)
- 3/4 cup cilantro, stems removed, chopped
- 2 cloves garlic, finely chopped or pressed
- 2 to 3 tablespoons lime juice (juice from whole limes)
- 1 tablespoon olive oil
- 1/4 teaspoon kosher salt (or any salt available)
- 4 12" x 12" aluminum foil sheets
- 1 cup water

Directions

Grease middle of each foil with olive oil.

Place fillets, skin side down, in center of foil, over the olive oil. Combine cilantro, garlic, lime juice, olive oil, and salt in a small bowl. Pour 1/4 of the mixture over each salmon filet.

Make packets around the filets and seal all edges tightly. Add the water to the cooker then add a rack or trivet.

Place the packets on the trivet. If you do not have a trivet or rack place them directly in. Make sure they are sealed tightly so no water gets through

Set the timer for 4 minutes and seal the pressure valve. When the cooking time is up release pressure manually. Carefully remove the hot packets.

Cut open and serve. Serves 3-4

Salmon with Pineapple, Strawberry, Mango Salas and Orange Lentals

Ingredients:

- 1¼ cup low-sodium chicken broth
- 1 cup orange juice
- ¾ cup green lentils
- ½ cup carrot, finely diced
- ¼ cup red onion, finely diced
- ¼ cup celery, finely diced
- 1 tbsps. honey
- 6 (4-5oz) salmon fillets, scaled and pin bones removed
- 1 tsp lemon juice

Salsa:

- 3/4 cup finely diced pineapple
- 3/4 cup finely diced mango
- 1/2 cup finely diced strawberries
- 1/4 cup finely diced red onion
- 2 Tbsp. chopped fresh mint (2 tsp dried)
- 2 Tbsp. orange juice
- 1 Tbsp. lime juice
- 1/4 tsp salt

Directions

Combine all ingredients except the salmon and lemon juice together in the pressure cooker and stir.

Place 1 sheet of parchment paper over the lentils in the pressure cooker.

Season salmon lightly with salt and pepper and place it on the parchment (skin-side down).

Close and lock the lid and set the timer for 8 minutes. Seal the pressure valve.

While the salmon is cooking, combine all of the salsa ingredients and set aside to give the flavors a chance to combine.

When the cooking time is done, release pressure manually and remove it by lifting out parchment.

Stir the lemon juice into the lentils and season with salt and pepper to taste.

Serve with about ½ a cup of lentils on a plate and top with a salmon fillet and 1/3 cup of salsa.

Serves 4-6

Steamed Fish Fillets

Ingredients

- 6-8 lg. flounder or cod fillets (fresh or frozen)
- 1 sm. bell pepper, sliced into thin rings
- 1 sm. onion, sliced into thin rings
- Salt to taste
- Lemon pepper to taste
- 1 tablespoon olive oil
- Aluminum foil squares (lg. enough to wrap individual fillets)

Directions

Rinse and pat dry fish fillets. Season very well. Place each fillet on a piece of aluminum foil.

Brush olive oil over the top of the salmon pieces.

Cover fillets with onion and bell pepper slices. Wrap each fillet in the foil. Make sure it is sealed tightly. Place individual foil packets on a trivet in pressure cooker with 2 cups of water. Close and lock the lid.

Seal the pressure valve. Set the timer for 4 minutes.

When the cooking time is up release the pressure manually remove the packets and serve.

Sticky Asian Salmon

Ingredients

- 2 (5 ounce/portions) boned salmon steaks or fillets (skin on or off)
- 1 teaspoon grated fresh ginger
- 1 teaspoon grated fresh garlic
- ½ small red chili, minced or finely diced (de-veined to reduce heat if desired)
- 1 tablespoon runny honey
- 1 tablespoon soy sauce
- 1 teaspoon sesame oil

Directions

Mix together all ingredients, except the salmon, to make a marinade. Coat the salmon in the marinade, cover, and refrigerate for at least 2 to 3 hours.

Put 1 cup of water and a trivet in the pressure cooker.

Remove the salmon from the marinade, put the fish onto foil sheets and seal all sides.

Set the remaining marinade aside for later use.

Place the packets on the trivet, close the lid and set the timer for 4 minutes. Release pressure manually. Remove the packets and carefully remove the salmon.

On the stovetop, heat a skillet, over medium heat until sizzling hot.

Brush the salmon with the remaining marinade and sear to caramelize, slightly char the surface, several minutes a side.

Serve immediately

Asian-Style Seafood Soup

Prep Time: *15 minutes*

Servings: *6*

Ingredients:

- 1 lbs. red snapper fillet
- ½ lbs. raw shrimp, peeled and deveined
- 1 tbsp. coconut oil
- 2 tbsp. minced ginger
- 1 tsp. minced garlic
- 1 cup sliced mushrooms
- 2 shredded carrots
- 3 cups water
- 3 cups clam juice
- 4 scallions, sliced
- 2 stalks lemongrass, minced
- 1 tbsp. fish sauce
- 1 cup chopped cilantro

Instructions:

Combine the carrots, mushrooms, water, clam juice, lemongrass, scallions and fish sauce in the cooker. Cover and lock the lid. Seal the pressure valve. Set the timer for 5 minutes.

When the cooking time is up, release the pressure manually. Open the lid.

Heat the oil in a skillet over medium heat. Add the garlic and ginger and cook for 1 minute. Stir in the fish and shrimp and cook for 1 to

2 minutes. Spoon the seafood into the pressure cooker and lock the lid. Set the timer for 6 minutes. Release pressure manually. Discard the lemon grass and stir in the cilantro to serve.

Shrimp and Scallop Stew

Prep Time: *10 minutes*

Servings: *4*

Ingredients:

- ¾ lbs. raw shrimp, peeled and deveined
- ¾ lbs. raw sea scallops
- 2 tbsp. olive oil
- 2 chopped leeks, white and light green parts only
- 1 ½ cups chopped tomatoes
- 1 carrot, diced
- 3 cloves garlic, minced
- 1 cup dry white wine
- 1 tsp. ground cumin
- ¼ tsp. cayenne pepper
- ¼ cup fresh chopped cilantro

Instructions:

Heat the oil in the pressure cooker. Add the leeks and garlic and sauté for, about 3 minutes.

Add the tomatoes, carrot, white wine and spices. Cover and lock the lid. Seal the pressure valve.

Set the timer for 5 minutes. When the cooking time is up release the pressure manually. Open lid. Stir in the shrimp and scallops and cook on heat until opaque, about 10 minutes or less.

Turn off the heat and stir in the cilantro to serve.

Spicy Fish Stew

Prep Time: *15 minutes*

Servings: 6

Ingredients:

- 2 lbs. cod fillets, cut into chunks
- ¼ cup olive oil
- 2 tsp. minced garlic
- 1 tsp. lemon zest
- ¾ tsp. red pepper flakes
- 3 red peppers, chopped
- 2 (14.5 oz.) cans chopped tomatoes
- 1 cup chopped green onion
- ½ cup chopped cilantro

Instructions:

Combine the peppers and tomatoes in the pressure cooker. Whisk together the oil, garlic, lemon zest and red pepper flakes then pour into the pressure cooker.

Close and lock the lid. Seal the pressure valve and set the timer for 5 minutes.

When the time is up release the pressure manually. Open the lid.

Add the fish and set the timer for another 5 minutes. Again release the pressure manually.

Open the lid and spoon into bowls and garnish with cilantro and green onion to serve.

Ginger Shrimp and Scallops Soup

Prep Time: *10 minutes*

Servings: *2*

Ingredients:

- ¼ lbs. uncooked shrimp
- ¼ lbs. raw scallops
- 2 Portobello mushrooms, sliced
- 1 cup sliced shitake mushrooms
- ½ cup sliced ginger root
- ½ cup chopped green onion
- ¼ cup chopped cilantro

Instructions:

Combine the stock and ginger in the pressure cooker. Close and lock the lid and set timer for 10 minutes.

Seal the pressure valve. When the cooking time is up release the pressure manually. Open the lid.

Spoon the ginger out of the pressure cooker and add the mushrooms, shrimp, scallops and green onions. Cover and set the timer for 5 additional minutes. Release pressure manually. Open the lid and stir in the cilantro and green onions just before serving. (If shrimp and scallops are not cooked thru let simmer for 3 additional minutes.

Shrimp and Sausage Stew

Prep Time: *10 minutes*

Servings: 6 to 8

Ingredients:

- 3 tbsp. olive oil
- 2 lbs. shell-on shrimp, raw
- 1 lbs. Andouille sausage, sliced
- 2 cups chopped tomatoes
- 1 onion, chopped
- 1 stalk celery, chopped
- ½ red pepper, chopped
- 1 tbsp. minced garlic
- 1 cup chicken stock
- ¼ cup chopped parsley
- ¼ tsp. cayenne pepper

Instructions:

Set the pressure cooker to the heat mode and add the oil. Stir in the garlic and cayenne and cook for 1 minute. Add the sausage and cook for 5 minutes or until lightly browned. Add the tomatoes and the stock.

Stir in the shrimp, and half the parsley into the cooker. Cover and set the timer for 6 minutes.

Release the pressure manually. Turn off the heat and serve with remaining parsley.

Sweet and Sour Scallop Soup

Prep Time: *15 minutes*

Servings: 4 to 6

Ingredients:

- 2 lbs. raw sea scallops
- 2 tbsp. olive oil
- 2 tbsp. coconut oil
- 2 cups sliced mushrooms
- ½ cup bamboo shoots
- ½ cup chopped green onion
- 4 large eggs, beaten
- 8 cups chicken stock
- ½ cup water
- 1/3 cup tapioca starch
- ¼ cup coconut aminos
- ¼ cup rice wine vinegar
- 1 tbsp. sesame oil

Instructions:

Combine all ingredients except for the eggs, scallops and coconut oil in the pressure cooker. Cook in heat or sauté mode until the vegetables are tender. Beat the eggs in a bowl then drizzle into the pressure cooker. Cook until the egg is cooked through. Add the scallops and coconut oil and cook for 5 more minutes or until scallops are cooked. Spoon the scallops into bowls and ladle the soup over them.

Cajun Oyster Stew

Prep Time: *20 minutes*

Servings: 6 to 8

Ingredients:

- 6 slices bacon, chopped
- 4 tbsp. coconut oil
- 1 tbsp. minced garlic
- 1 cup chopped onion
- ½ cup chopped celery
- ½ cup green onions, chopped
- 1 quart oysters, liquid reserved
- 3 cups almond milk
- ½ cup chopped parsley
- ½ cup canned coconut milk
- ½ cup almond flour
- ¼ cup dry white wine
- ½ tsp. ground white pepper
- Pinch cayenne pepper

Instructions:

Drain the oysters and pour the liquid into the pressure cooker. Add the garlic, onion, celery, green onion, parsley and white wine. Cover and set timer for 5 minutes. Whisk in the coconut milk and cook for an additional 10 minutes in the heat or sauté mode.

Meanwhile, cook the bacon in a skillet until crisp then spoon out onto paper towels to drain.

Add the coconut oil to the skillet and stir in the white pepper and cayenne. Toss the oysters in the almond flour and add to the skillet.

Cook until softened, about 5 minutes. Stir in the green onions, garlic, white pepper and cayenne. Cook for 1 minute. Ladle the soup into bowls and top with oysters and bacon.

Lobster Coconut Soup

....

Prep Time: *5 minutes*

Servings: 4

Ingredients:

- 2 cooked lobster tails
- 1 tbsp. coconut oil
- 4 cups seafood stock
- 1 cup coconut milk
- 1 cup sliced mushrooms
- 2 chopped green onions
- 1 tbsp. chopped cilantro
- 2 tbsp. lime juice
- 1 tbsp. lime zest

Instructions:

Scoop the lobster meat from the shell then slice and set aside. Combine the remaining ingredients in the pressure cooker. Close and lock the lid, seal the pressure valve and set the timer for 5 minutes.

When the cooking time is up release pressure manually. Open the lid.

Stir in the lobster and simmer for 5 minutes. Serve hot.

Hot and Sour Shrimp Soup

Prep Time: *10 minutes*

Servings: *4 to 6*

Ingredients:

- 1 lbs. raw shrimp, with peel
- 1 tsp. olive oil
- 8 cups chicken stock
- 2 tsp. fresh grated ginger
- 4 cloves garlic, minced
- 4 shallots, sliced
- 4 Serrano peppers, minced
- ¼ cup fish sauce
- ¼ cup fresh cilantro leaves
- ¼ cup chopped basil leaves
- 1/3 cup fresh lime juice
- 1 tsp. black pepper

Instructions:

Peel the shrimp and reserve the shells. Toss the shrimp in the oil and chill for 1 hour.

Combine the chicken stock, shrimp shells, garlic and ginger in the pressure cooker.

Cover and set timer for 10 minutes. Release pressure manually and open lid.

Strain the mixture and discard the solids.

Return the liquid to the cooker. Add the fish sauce, shallots and Serrano peppers.

Stir in the cilantro, basil, lime juice and pepper and the shrimp then cover and set timer for 5 minutes.

When the cooking time is up, release the pressure manually. Open the lid and save.

Cajun Fish with Peppers Stew

Prep Time: *5 minutes*

Servings: *2*

Ingredients:

- 10 oz. halibut, cut into 1-inch chunks
- 1 tbsp. coconut oil
- 1 tsp. minced garlic
- ½ cup chopped red onion
- 1 (12 oz.) jar roasted red peppers, chopped
- 1 (14.5 oz.) can diced tomatoes
- ¼ cup fresh chopped cilantro
- 1 tbsp. lemon juice
- ½ tsp. red pepper flakes
- ½ tsp. black pepper
- Dash cayenne pepper
- ½ cup of water

Instructions:

Heat the oil in the pressure cooker in the heat or sauté mode. Stir in the garlic and red pepper flakes.

Cook for 1 minute then stir in the tomatoes and chopped peppers. Cook for 3 minutes then add the water. Add the onions and spices. Stir in the lemon juice and cilantro then add the fish. Close and lock the lid. Seal the pressure valve and set the timer for 5 minutes. When the time is up release pressure manually. Serve hot.

GRAINS

Cheese Pasta Casserole

Ingredients

- 1 lb rigatoni, ziti or penne pasta
- 1 lb ground beef
- 1 medium onion, finely chopped
- 1 medium carrot, finely chopped
- 1 medium celery stalk, finely chopped
- 3 oz red wine
- 2 cups tomato puree
- 14 oz mozzarella cheese, diced or shredded
- Butter
- 2 tsp salt
- Freshly ground black pepper

Procedure

Heat 2 Tbs butter

Saute onions, carrots and celery

Add ground beef

Add 1/2 tsp salt and ground pepper Stir and brown beef into small pieces Add wine and wait a few moments

Add pasta, tomato puree and 2 tsp of salt

Add enough water to cover the pasta

Close and lock lid to cooker and set for 5 minutes

Release pressure

Stir and allow to sit for a minute or so Divide and pour into an oiled casserole dish Sprinkle half the cheese on top

Pour remaining pasta mix on top and add cheese to that

Place pads of butter on top

Place in over on broil for 3 minutes until cheese has melted and is turning brown

Allow to rest for 5 minutes and serve

Cuban Black Beans

Ingredients

- Small piece of salt pork, diced
- 2 cups black beans, uncooked
- 3 cups of water
- 3 Tbs olive oil
- 1 medium onion, chopped
- 1 small green pepper, chopped
- 4 garlic cloves, chopped
- 1/2 tsp ground cumin
- 1/4 chopped cilantro
- 2 bay leaves
- 3 Tbs wine
- Salt and pepper

Procedure

Heat oil in open cooker

Add diced pork stir fry until browned

Add onions, green peppers and cook until onions are translucent

Add garlic and spices, and cilantro

Add wine

Add beans and water

Close lid and lock Set for 45 minutes Release pressure

Serve alone, as a side or on top of rice.

Pressure Cooked Mexican Beans

Ingredients

- 1 Tbs vegetable oil
- 1 onion, chopped
- 1 bunch cilantro stems and leaves divided and chopped
- ¼ tsp chile powder
- 1/2 tsp cumin
- 2 cups dry beans
- 2 cups water
- 1 tsp salt

Procedure

Heat oil in open cooker

Saute onion, cilantro, cumin until onion is translucent

Add beans and water

Close and lock lid

Set for 45 minutes

Release pressure and mash beans

Serve with sour cream dollop

Red Beans and Rice

Ingredients

- 1 lb dry red beans
- 1 large yellow onion, diced
- 1 cup diced celery
- 1 cup chopped green pepper
- 4 garlic cloves, finely chopped
- 4 bay leaves
- 4 Tbs parsley, chopped
- 2 tsp dried thyme, crushed
- 1 1/2 teaspoons salt
- 1/2 tsp crushed red pepper
- 1 tsp freshly ground black pepper
- 3/4 cup olive oil
- 4 cups water
- 2 cups rice

Procedure

Rinse beans

Place onion, celery, green pepper, garlic and bay leaves in bowl and set aside

Add olive oil to bowl and let sit for 30 minutes

Pour vegetables over beans, let sit 10 minutes more Be sure the beans are covered, add water if needed Add rice and stir

Close and lock lid

Set for 45 minutes

Remove bay leaves and serve

If additional cooking time is required, replace lid and add 5 -10 minutes at a time

Risotto and Chorizo

Ingredients

- 1 small white onion, minced
- 1 cup minced sweet chorizo
- 1 tbs. olive oil
- ¾ cup Arborio rice
- 1 cup dry red wine
- 2 cups chicken stock, warm
- 1 cups grated parmesan cheese
- 2 tbs. butter
- 1 cup peas, frozen, fresh or canned

Procedure

Heat chorizo in open cooker Remove chorizo and leave fat Add olive oil and onions

Cook until onion are translucent

Add rice stir until it changes color (3 to 4 minutes) Add wine and cook until reduced

Add stock

Close and lock lid Set for 5 minutes Release pressure

Mix in butter, cheese, peas, herbs, and chorizo

Salt and pepper to taste

Spinach Pesto Pasta

Ingredients

- 1 lb. of pasta
- 1 lb. spinach, chopped (fresh or frozen)
- 4 garlic cloves (2 smashed, 2 finely chopped or pressed)
- 1/4 cup or 2 oz. pine nuts, whole or chopped
- 2 tsp. sea salt
- Extra virgin olive oil
- ½ cup pecorino Romano cheese, grated

Preparation

Set the pressure cooker to heat or sauté and heat the olive oil.

Add smashed garlic cloves and spinach (stir occasionally) Cook until spinach is soft and wilted.

Add pasta, salt and enough water to cover the pasta. Smooth out to an even layer.

Close and lock the lid. Set the timer for 6 minutes.

Seal the pressure valve. When the cooking time is up release the pressure manually.

Open the lid. Add finely chopped garlic, stir and let set.

Divide into bowls and top each with pine nuts, a swirl of olive oil and dust with cheese

VEGETABLES

Asparagus with Garlic and Tomatoes

Ingredients

- 16 thick white or green asparagus spears
- 1 tsp sugar
- ½ tsp salt
- 3 large red salad tomatoes
- 8 thin slices of Serrano ham or prosciutto
- 2 hard-boiled eggs finely minced
- 2 cloves garlic, minced
- 1 sprig of parsley, minced
- Extra-virgin olive oil
- Salt to taste

Preparation

Cut tomatoes into ½ inch slices

Cut off the woody ends of the asparagus spears, peel the exterior portions

Place asparagus in a steamer basket and place the basket in the pressure cooker. Add the teaspoon of sugar, 1/2 teaspoon of salt and one cup of water.

Close and lock lid set timer for 3 minutes.

Release quickly and drain the asparagus.

Heat oil in a skillet and brown tomato slices.

Season with salt and sprinkle with parsley and garlic, cook for one minute more.

Arrange on a serving platter.

Make a roll of each slice of ham.

Arrange ham rolls on tomato slices.

Place asparagus in center of platter and garnish with boiled eggs

No-Bake Baked Potato

Ingredients

- 10 small baking potatoes
- 2 cups of water

Preparation

Add 2 cups of water to pressure cooker

Clean and wrap each potato in foil

Layer foil wrapped potatoes in cooker on metal trivet

Close and lock lid

Set on high for 15 minutes.

Let pressure release on its own

Brussels sprouts with Bacon

Ingredients

- ½ cup bacon, diced
- 1 lbs. Brussels sprouts, trimmed and cut in half
- 1 Tbs. Dijon mustard
- 1 cup chicken or vegetable broth
- 2 Tbs. fresh chopped dill
- 1 Tbs. butter

Preparation

Set the pressure cooker to heat and cook the bacon

Add Brussels sprouts

Add mustard and chicken broth

Close the lid and lock

Set the timer for 4 minutes

When done release the pressure manually

Add dill, butter and season with salt and pepper to taste

Cabbage and Bacon

Ingredients

- 1 head of Cabbage- cored
- 3 slices of bacon
- 1/4 cup butter
- 2 cups of chicken broth
- Salt and pepper to taste

Procedure

Chop cored cabbage into 2" sections

Cook bacon in an open pressure cooker 4 to 5 minutes

Do not crisp the bacon unless you just like it that way.

Add butter and stir until melted.

Place the chopped cabbage into the pot and pour in chicken broth.

Add salt and black pepper to taste and toss the cabbage until coated.

Close and lock the pressure cooker lid set for 3 minutes

Release pressure naturally and serve hot

Smothered Cabbage and Greens

Ingredients

- 1 head of cabbage
- Small bunch of greens of your choice
- 1/2 large onion
- 1/2 lb. bacon
- 1 tsp. oil
- Salt and pepper

Procedure

Core and chop cabbage Clean and chop greens Chop onion

Crisp bacon in open cooker

Stir in greens, onion, and salt/pepper to taste

Close and lock lid, set for 15 minutes

Release pressure manually and serve

Candied Yams with Orange Zest

Ingredients

- 1 cup orange juice
- 2 large sweet potatoes
- Salt to taste
- 1/2 cup brown sugar
- 1 tsp. grated orange peel
- 2 Tbs. butter

Preparation

Place orange juice in cooker

Peel yams and place in basket in cooker

Season with salt, brown sugar, and orange zest

Place a small amount of butter on dish

Close lid and lock in place Set timer for 7 minutes Release pressure manually Lift out yams

Thicken sauce in heated cooer and pour over yams

Carrots with Crumb Topping

Ingredients

- 3 tablespoon butter
- ¼ cup dry breadcrumbs
- 1 tsp. lemon juice
- 1 Tbs. parsley minced
- 1 lb. carrots cut in 2" sticks
- Salt

Preparation

Melt the butter in the cooker

Add the bread crumbs and cook until they are golden and crunchy.

Stir in lemon juice and parsley Transfer to a small bowl. Set aside. Add 1 ¾ cups water to clean cooker.

Arrange the carrots in the cooker basket, sprinkle salt and place in cooker.

Close and lock lid and set timer for 5 minutes Release pressure manually and remove the lid. Lift out the cooker basket and let drain.

Spoon the crumb mixture over the carrots and serve.

Eggplant Dip

Ingredients

- 2 lbs. eggplant
- 1/4 cup olive oil
- 1 teaspoon salt
- ½ cup water
- 4 cloves garlic with the skin on (reserve one to use fresh at the end)
- 1/4 cup of lemon juice
- 1 Tbs. tahini
- 1 bunch of thyme
- Olive oil
- 3 black olives

Procedure

Peel the eggplant by alternating stripes of skin and no skin.

Slice chunks to cover the bottom of your open cooker.

Add the 1/4 cup of olive oil and heat.

Place the large chunks of eggplant "face down" to fry and caramelize on one side.

Add garlic cloves with the skin on. Flip over eggplant.

Add the remaining uncooked eggplant on top and the salt and water.

Close and lock. Set timer for 3 minutes and release pressure naturally.

Fish out the garlic cloves and remove their skin and chop.

Add the Tahini, lemon juice, and finely chopped garlic. Mix contents well.

Pour into serving dish and sprinkle with fresh

Thyme, black olives and fresh olive oil and serving.

Eggplant

Ingredients

- 2 large eggplants, cubed
- 1 garlic clove, smashed
- 2 anchovies
- 1 bunch of fresh oregano (or 1 tablespoon dry)
- Hot pepper flakes to taste
- Salt and pepper

Preparation

Cube the eggplant.

Sprinkle the cubes with salt.

Add a plate on top of the cubed eggplant to rest for half an hour

Heat olive oil, garlic clove and a pinch of pepper, the oregano and anchovies

Remove garlic clove

Separate eggplant into two halves

Add half to cooker, add salt and pepper to taste

Brown one half of eggplant

Add rest of eggplant and clove of garlic

Mix well

Close and lock lid, set timer for 5 minutes

Release pressure and move to serving dish

Italian Green Beans

Ingredients

- 1 pound fresh green beans, snapped
- 2 cups fresh cherry tomatoes
- 1/2 cup water
- 1 clove garlic
- 1 Tbsp. olive oil
- 1 sprig fresh basil
- Salt and pepper to taste-buds

Preparation

Heat olive oil in pressure cooker and sauté garlic until lightly toasted. Add tomatoes and water. Add green beans, salt and pepper, and basil.

Put on the lid, lock it down, close the vent and set the timer for 16 minutes.

When time is up release pressure manually and remove the lid.

Serve as a side dish with Italian Sausages.

Mashed Potato with Herbs

Ingredients

- 3 large potatoes, peeled and cubed
- 1 cup chicken broth
- 1 cup warm skim milk
- 2 Tbs. olive oil
- 1 Tbs. minced thyme
- 1/2 tsp. garlic powder
- 1/2 tsp. dried rosemary, crushed
- 1/2 tsp. salt
- 1/4 tsp. pepper
- 3 cloves of garlic, minced

Procedure

Add potatoes to cooker Add garlic and broth Close and lock lid

Set timer for 6 minutes

Release pressure

Drain off broth leaving only 1/4 cup

Add milk and olive oil

Beat until fluffy Add salt, pepper, Garnish herbs and serve

Roasted New Potatoes

Ingredients

- 5 Tbs. vegetable oil
- 2 lbs. baby or fingerling potatoes
- 1 sprig rosemary
- 3 garlic cloves unpeeled
- 1/2 cup stock
- Salt and pepper

Preparation

Heat oil in open cooker

Add potatoes, garlic and rosemary

Brown outside of potatoes Place small slit in each potato Add stock

Close lid and lock

Set timer for 9 minutes

Release pressure manually

Peel garlic cloves, serve crushed or whole as you like

Salt and pepper to taste and serve

Stir Fry Broccoli

Ingredients

- 2 Tbs. sesame, olive or peanut oil
- 1 large clove garlic lightly crushed and peeled
- 1 slice fresh ginger
- 1 bunch broccoli, trimmed, cut into flowerets
- Salt to taste
- ½ cup of chicken stock or water
- 2 Tbs. soy sauce

Procedure

Place oil in open cooker, heat

Add broccoli and stir fry until bright green

Add salt, ginger, and garlic Place in steamer basket Add stock and soy sauce

Place steamer in cooker, close lid and lock

Set timer for 4 minutes

Release pressure manually

Serve as is or with liquid as sauce

Stuffed Cabbage Logs

Ingredients

- 8 cabbage leaves
- 1 lb. ground beef
- 1/2 cup uncooked rice
- 2 small cans of tomato sauce
- 3 tsp. of ground red pepper (chili powder)
- 2 cloves of chopped garlic
- 1/2 cup chopped onion
- Salt and pepper to taste
- 2 10 oz. cans of diced tomatoes with chili peppers

Preparation

Soften cabbage leaves in boiling water

Mix ground beef, rice, tomato sauce, chili powder, garlic, onion, salt and black pepper in bowl,

Divide the meat mixture into 8 portions and place the meat on the softened cabbage leaves.

Roll the leaves up to form logs and tuck the edges under the logs

Place in cooker, close and lock lid, set timer for 25 minutes

Use quick release for pressure

Pour diced tomatoes and green chili peppers over rolls and serve immediately

Baked Sweet Potato Stuffed With Beans & Greens

Ingredients

- 4 sweet potatoes
- 2 tablespoons olive oil
- 1 shallot, diced
- 1 garlic clove, minced
- 1 (4-inch) sprig fresh rosemary
- 1/4 teaspoon red pepper flakes
- 1 1/2 cups (or 1 can) cooked and drained white beans
- 6 cups kale, trimmed and sliced into ribbons
- Juice of 1/4 lemon
- Salt and freshly ground black pepper

Preparation

Scrub the sweet potatoes wrap in foil

Place them on a metal trivet in cooker

Place beans and greens in metal container in cooker

Add to beans and greens the shallots, garlic, rosemary and red pepper. Salt and pepper to taste

Set pressure cooker to 15 minutes and close and lock lid

Allow steam to dissipate naturally. Add lemon and remove Rosemary

Slice potatoes and add beans and green mix. Serve and enjoy

Texas Style Cabbage

Ingredients

- Small head of cabbage
- 6 slices of bacon
- 2 fresh jalapenos, sliced and seeded
- 5 tsp corn meal
- 1/2 onion chopped
- 1/4 tsp. Cheyenne
- 1 tsp. sweetener or sugar
- Salt and Pepper to taste

Procedure

Chop bacon and brown in open cooker

Stir in onion and jalapeno

Add cabbage with sweetener, salt - pepper and Cheyenne

Close and lock lid, set timer for 15 minutes

Release pressure manually and serve

Orange Spiced Sweet Potatoes

SERVES 4

Ingredients

- 2lbs. sweet potatoes peeled and diced
- ½ cup of dark brown sugar (packed)
- 1 stick of butter cut into small pieces
- 1 tsp. ground cinnamon
- ½ teaspoon of ground nutmeg
- ½ tsp. grated orange peel
- 1 cup of orange juice
- ¼ tsp of salt
- 1 tsp. vanilla

Directions

Place the orange juice, vanilla, nutmeg, salt and peel into the pressure cooker.

Add the sweet potato pieces and mix.

Close and lock the lid and set the timer for 20 minutes.

Release the pressure manually and remove the lid. Mash the sweet potato with a hand mixer, potato

masher, or electric mixer.

Add ¼ cup of milk or whipping cream for smooth mixture.

Sprinkle with a mixture of the brown sugar and cinnamon

DESERT S

Apple Brown Betty

Ingredients

- 1 cup graham cracker crumbs
- 1/4 cup butter, melted
- 3/4 cup brown sugar
- 1 tsp. cinnamon
- 1/4 tsp. nutmeg
- 1 tsp. vanilla
- 3 apples chopped
- 1/2 cup raisins

Procedure

Mix cracker crumbs and melted butter and set aside

Combine brown sugar, cinnamon, nutmeg and vanilla and set aside

Combine chopped apples and raisins; set aside

Grease a bowl that fits into the cooker

Layer with 1/3 of the crumb mixture and 1/2 of the apple mixture

Top with sugar mixture

Repeat layers ending with crumbs on top

Cover bowl with aluminum foil

Pour 2/3 cup of water into cooker

Place rack in cooker and set bowl on top

Close and lock lid

Set timer for 15 minutes

Release pressure manually

Cool and serve chilled. Top with whipped cream

Apple Sauce

Ingredients

- 3 lbs. apples, peeled, cored, and quartered
- 3/4 tsp. ground cinnamon
- 1 cup water or apple juice
- Lemon juice
- Lemon zest
- Honey

Procedure

Place the apples, cinnamon, and water (or juice) in cooker

Lock the lid in place

Set timer for 5 minutes

Release pressure

Puree in blender or food processor

Stir in lemon zest, honey and or lemon juice to taste

Serve warm or chill

Caramel Pudding, Flan, Dip

Ingredient

- 1 can Sweet Condensed Milk

Procedure

Place trivet in cooker

Place can of condensed milk in steamer basket

Cover can completely with water

Close and lock lid

Set for 20 min

Unplug cooker to release pressure slowly

Allow to cool over night

Once cool you may open and use or store can as is

Once open you can freeze left over for up to 3 months

Cinnamon Raisin Bread Pudding

Ingredients

- 4 cups cubed French bread
- 1 cup raisins
- 1 cup milk
- 1 cup evaporated milk
- 2 large eggs
- 1 egg yolk
- 1/4 cup sugar
- 1/8 tsp. gr. cinnamon
- 1/8 tsp. gr nutmeg
- 1/2 Tbs. butter
- 2 1/2 cups water

Procedure

Place bread in insert pan

Mix raisins through out

Combine evaporated milk, milk, eggs, sugar, and spices in mixing bowl

Whip until frothy with whisk or fork

Pour mixture over bread

Make sure bread is submerged

On a piece of foil, large enough to cover the baking insert, rub butter in circle

Cover with butter side down and wrap tightly

Place insert in cooker

Close and lock lid

Set timer for 15 minutes

Release pressure naturally

Remove foil and stir, serve warm with Rum sauce

Custard

Ingredients

- 2 cups milk
- 2 eggs
- 1/3 cup sugar
- 1/2 tsp. vanilla
- 1 cup water

Procedure

Scald milk in sauce pan and allow to cool

Add eggs and sugar

Add milk slowly stirring constantly

Add vanilla extract

Pour into individual custard cups Cover cups with aluminum foil Add water to pressure cooker

Place trivet and steamer basket into cooker

Place foil-covered custard cups in steamer basket. Close and lock lid

Set timer for 8 minutes Release pressure and cool Serve chilled

Lemon Pudding

Ingredients

- 1/2 cup sugar
- 2 Tbs. flour
- 1/8 tsp. salt
- 1 Tbs. butter
- 3 Tbs. lemon juice
- Rind of 1 lemon, grated
- 2 egg yolks, beaten
- 2 egg whites, beaten
- 2/3 cup milk
- 2 cups water

Procedure

Separate eggs

Beat egg yolks to a light lemony color

In separate bowl, beat egg whites to a soft peak. Combine flour, sugar, salt and butter

Add lemon juice and rind, beaten egg yolks, and milk. Mix

Fold in beaten egg whites

Pour into individual custard cups Cover each with aluminum foil. Pour water into pressure cooker Place cups on rack inside cooker Close and lock lid

Set timer for 10 minutes

Release pressure

Serve warm or cold with whipped cream.

Pears in Wine

Ingredients

- 4 large pears, peeled
- 1 bottle (26-ounce) Beaujolais wine or grape juice
- 1 (12-ounce) jar currant jelly
- 1 lemon
- 2 sprigs rosemary
- 1/2 vanilla bean
- 4 whole cloves
- 4 whole black peppercorns

Procedure

Core the pears from bottom leaving stems in tact

Place wine and jelly in open cooker to melt

Peel strips of lemon and add to wine

Add juice of lemon to cooker

Cut foil in 12 inch squares (4)

Dip pears in liquid and place on foil

Wrap pears and secure at top Add remaining ingredients Arrange pears on rack in cooker

Close and lock lid, set timer for 8 minutes

Release pressure manually, remove pears and pour hot liquid over pears.

Chill for 24 hours before serving

Pumpkin Pie

Ingredients

- 1 1/2 cups cooked pumpkin, mashed
- 1 cup sugar or Splenda
- 1/2 tsp. cinnamon
- 1/2 tsp. ground ginger
- 1/2 tsp. ground cloves
- 1/2 tsp. salt
- 1 1/2 cups evaporated milk
- 1/2 cup milk
- 2 eggs

Procedure

Cut the pumpkin into 1-2 inch slices

Place water, trivet, and then steamer basket in pressure cooker

Place pumpkin in steamer basket

Close and lock lid

Set timer for 10 minutes Release pressure manually Mash cooked pumpkin

Combine all remaining ingredients in a bowl with pumpkin

Whip until smooth

Pour into 8" baking dish lined with pastry

(homemade or frozen)

Bake at 425F for 10 minutes

Lower heat to 300 and bake another 45 minutes until filling is firm

Electric Pressure Cooker Dump Recipes

Most of these recipes are quick and easy, just prep the ingredients, place in the pressure cooker, set the timer, release the pressure and you'll have a great healthy meal. Check them out and don't be afraid to add or change ingredients to you own taste. Also get familiar with your own pressure cooker and the time it takes to cook different foods and adjust if necessary. Unfortunately, not all electric pressure cookers operate the same, some have different controls and cooking times could be slightly different. One you get the knack of your particular electric pressure cooker the possibilities are endless

Caribbean Dump Chicken

Ingredients

- 8 oz. pineapple chunks in juice
- 1/4 cup brown sugar
- 1/2 teaspoon nutmeg
- 1/3 cup orange juice
- 1/2 cup golden raisins
- 1 1/2 lbs. cut up chicken

Procedure

Put chicken in the bottom of the pressure cooker pot. Pour remaining ingredients over the chicken.

Close and lock the lid and set timer for 12 minutes. Seal the pressure valve.

When the time is up release the pressure manually. Open the lid and serve the chicken with the sauce.

Barbecued Pot Roast

Ingredients

- 2 lb pot roast
- 1 tsp salt
- 1/2 cup tomato paste
- 24 peppercorns
- 1 onion, chopped
- 1 tsp Worcestershire sauce
- I cup water

Procedure

Sprinkle salt over the roast and place in pressure cooker. Pour in water. Spread tomato paste over meat. Imbed peppercorns into paste. Top with onions and Worcestershire sauce. Cover and set timer for 45 minutes. Release pressure manually. Serve meat with accumulated gravy.

Chinese Ribs

Ingredients

- 1/4 cup soy sauce
- 1/4 cup orange marmalade
- 2 tbs ketchup
- 1 clove garlic, crushed
- 3 to 4 lbs. country-style spareribs
- 2 cups water

Procedure

Combine soy sauce, marmalade, ketchup and garlic. Brush on both sides of ribs. Add water to the pressure cooker Place in the ribs. Pour remaining sauce over all. Cover set timer for 40 minutes. Release pressure manually. Remove ribs and simmer sauce till it thickens. Makes 4 to 6 servings.

Herb Wine Dump Chicken

Ingredients

- 1 cup red wine
- 2/3 cup vegetable oil
- 2 cloves crushed garlic
- 1/2 lemon, sliced thinly
- 2 tablespoons minced parsley
- 1 teaspoon thyme
- 1 teaspoon basil
- 1/2 teaspoon salt
- 1/4 teaspoon pepper
- 1 1/2 lbs. chicken pieces

Procedure

Put chicken in the bottom of the pressure cooker. Pour remaining ingredients over the chicken. Close and lock the lid and set the timer for 12 minutes. Release the pressure manually. Serve hot with vegetables.

Creamy Chicken

Ingredients

- 1 can condensed cream of chicken soup
- 4-6 sliced mushrooms
- 1/2 chopped red onion
- 1 1/2 pounds skinless, boneless chicken breasts (cut into strips if you'd like)
- 1/4 cup white wine (optional)
- 1/2 cup water

Procedure

Put all in the pressure cooker. Close the lid and set the timer for 12 minutes.

Release the pressure manually. If the sauce is not thick enough, simmer in the pressure cooker with the lid off for 5 minutes.

Chili Chicken dump

Ingredients

- 4-6 boneless skinless chicken breasts
- 1 can of chilies
- 1 can of black beans, drained.
- packet of taco seasoning
- 3/4 jar of your favorite salsa
- 1 can of corn (optional)
- 1/2 cup water

Procedure

Add the water to the pressure cooker

Add all the remaining ingredients topped with the chicken breasts.

Set the timer for 12 minutes and then release pressure manually.

BBQ Jelly Chicken

Ingredients

- 3-4 chicken breasts
- 3/4 cup Ketchup
- 3/4 cup Blackberry Jam (Strawberry, peach, and apricot also work well)
- 1/4 cup White Vinegar
- 1 Teaspoons Worcestershire sauce
- 2 Teaspoons Chili Powder
- 1/8 Teaspoon Salt
- 1/2 cup water

Procedure

Add all ingredients to the pressure cooker, mix and close the lid. Set timer for 12 minutes. Release pressure manually.

Lemon Marinade Chicken

Ingredients

- 2-3 chicken breasts
- 2/3 cup Lemon Juice
- 1/4 cup Cider Vinegar
- 1/4 cup Vegetable Oil
- 2 Tablespoons Minced Onion

Procedure

Dump all ingredients into the pressure cooker, close the lid and set the timer for 12 minutes. Reduce the pressure manually. Serve hot with vegetables.

Savory Chicken

Ingredients

- 4-6 chicken breasts (boneless/skinless)
- 2 cans stewed tomatoes
- 4 tbs white wine
- 4 cloves minced garlic
- 1 lg onion
- 1 cup chicken broth
- 2 tbs salt
- *4c frozen broccoli

Procedure

Add all ingredients to the pressure cooker. Mix and close lid. Set the timer for 12 minutes. Release pressure manually.

French Chicken Stew

Ingredients

- 4 cups sliced button and/or stemmed shiitake mushrooms
- 1 14 1/2 ounce can diced tomatoes, undrained
- 2 medium carrots, thinly diagonally sliced
- 1 medium onion, chopped
- 1 medium red potato, cut into 1-inch pieces
- 1/2 cup fresh green beans, cut into 1-inch pieces
- 1/2 cup pitted ripe olives, halved
- 1 cup reduced-sodium chicken broth
- 1/2 cup dry white wine or chicken broth
- 2 tablespoons quick-cooking tapioca
- 1 teaspoon herbs de Provence or dried Italian
- seasoning, crushed
- 3/4 teaspoon dried thyme, crushed
- 1/4 teaspoon coarsely ground black pepper
- 8 skinless, boneless chicken thighs (1-3/4 to 2 lbs. total)
- 1/2 teaspoon seasoned salt
- 1 (14 ounce) jar tomato pasta sauce or one
- 16-ounce jar Alfredo pasta sauce
- French bread (optional)

Procedure

In a pressure cooker combine mushrooms, tomatoes, carrots, onion, potato, green beans, olives, broth, wine, tapioca, herbs de Provence, thyme, and pepper. Place chicken on top; sprinkle with seasoned salt.

Cover and set timer for 12 minutes. Release pressure manually. Open lid and stir in pasta sauce. Good served with French bread.

Cashew Chicken

Ingredients

- 1 (10 3/4 ounce) can condensed golden mushroom soup
- 1/2 cup water
- 3 tablespoons soy sauce
- 1 teaspoon ground ginger
- 1 1/2 lbs. chicken tenders
- 1 (16 ounce) package frozen broccoli stir-fry vegetable blend
- 1 (4 ounce) can (drained weight) sliced mushrooms
- 1/2 cup cashews
- Hot cooked brown rice* (optional)

Procedure

In the pressure cooker, combine mushroom soup, water, soy sauce, and ginger. Stir in chicken, stir-fry vegetables, and mushrooms.

Cover and set timer for 10 minutes. Release pressure manually. Open the lid and stir cashews into the chicken mixture.

Stir cashews into chicken mixture. Let sit for 5 minutes. If desired, serve over hot cooked rice.

Makes 6 servings.

Chicken Country Captain

Ingredients

- 1 medium sweet onion, cut into thin wedges
- 3 pounds chicken drumsticks and/or thighs, skin removed
- 1 medium green sweet pepper, cut into thin strips
- 1 medium yellow sweet pepper, cut into thin strips
- 1/4 cup currants or golden raisins
- 2 cloves garlic, minced
- 1 (14 oz.) can diced tomatoes, undrained
- 2 tablespoons quick cooking tapioca, crushed
- 2 teaspoons curry powder
- 1/2 teaspoon salt
- 1/2 teaspoon ground cumin
- 1/4 teaspoon ground mace
- 1/2 cup chicken broth
- Hot cooked rice
- 2 tablespoons chopped green onion
- 2 tablespoons sliced almonds, toasted

Procedure

In the pressure cooker, place onion, chicken, sweet peppers, currants, and garlic.

In a large bowl, combine undrained tomatoes, chicken broth, tapioca, curry powder, salt, cumin, and mace. Pour over the ingredients in the cooker.

Cover and set the timer for 12 minutes.

When the cooking time is up release the pressure manually.

Serve chicken mixture over rice.

Sprinkle with green onions and almonds.

In-a-Hurry Chicken Curry

Ingredients

- 1 1 oz. package frozen stew vegetables
- 4 large chicken thighs, skin removed (1 1/2 to 1 3/4 pounds)
- Salt and ground black pepper
- 1 (10 ¾) ounce can condensed cream of potato soup
- 1/4 cup water
- 2 teaspoons curry powder
- 1 tablespoon snipped fresh cilantro.

Procedure

Cut up the chicken to bite sized pieces.

Add all ingredient (chicken last) to the pressure cooker and close and lock the lid.

Seal the pressure valve.

Set the timer for 15 minutes.

Release the pressure manually when cooking time is up.

Easy Chicken Tetrazzini

Ingredients

- 2 1/2 pounds skinless, boneless chicken breast halves and/or thighs, cut into 1-inch pieces
- 2 4 1/2 ounce cans sliced mushrooms drained
- 1 16 oz. jar Alfredo pasta sauce
- 1/4 cup chicken broth or water
- 2 tablespoons dry sherry (optional)
- 1/4 teaspoon ground nutmeg
- 1/4 teaspoon ground black pepper
- 10 ounces dried spaghetti or linguine
- 2/3 cup grated Parmesan cheese
- 3/4 cup thinly sliced green onions (6)
- Toasted French bread slices (optional)

Procedure

Combine chicken and mushrooms in he pressure cooker. In a medium bowl stir together pasta sauce, broth, sherry (if desired), nutmeg, and pepper. Pour over mixture in cooker.

Cover and set timer for 12 minutes. Meanwhile, cook spaghetti according to package directions; drain. Reduce pressure manually and open the lid.

Stir cheese into chicken mixture. Serve over hot cooked spaghetti. Sprinkle each serving with green onion. Good served with French bread.

Hot and Spicy Braised Peanut Chicken

Ingredients

- 2 medium onions, cut into thin wedges
- 1 1/2 cups sliced carrot (3 medium)
- 1 small red sweet pepper, cut into bite-size strips
- 2 pounds skinless, boneless chicken thighs, cut into 1-inch pieces
- 3/4 cup chicken broth
- 3 tablespoons creamy peanut butter
- 1/2 teaspoon finely shredded lime peel
- 2 tablespoons lime juice
- 2 tablespoons soy sauce
- 2 tablespoons quick-cooking tapioca
- 2 teaspoons red curry paste
- 4 garlic, minced
- 1/2 cup unsweetened coconut milk
- 1 cup frozen peas
- Hot cooked rice
- Chopped peanuts (optional)
- Snipped fresh cilantro (optional)

Procedure

Place onions, carrot, and sweet pepper in the pressure cooker. Top with chicken. In a medium bowl, whisk together broth, peanut butter, lime peel, lime juice, soy sauce, tapioca, ginger, curry paste, and garlic until smooth. Pour over all in cooker.

Cover and set the timer for 12 minutes. Release the pressure manually and remove lid. Stir in coconut milk and peas. Let stand, uncovered, for 5 minutes.

Serve chicken mixture over hot cooked rice. If desired, sprinkle with chopped peanuts and cilantro. Makes 6 servings.

Sloppy Chicken Joes

Ingredients

- Nonstick cooking spray
- 3 lbs. uncooked ground chicken or uncooked ground turkey
- 2 14 ounce jars pizza sauce
- 2 cups frozen (yellow, green, and red) peppers and onion, stir-fry vegetables, thawed and chopped
- 1 14 1/2 ounce can diced tomatoes
- 8 hoagie rolls, split
- 8 slices mozzarella or provolone cheese

Procedure

Coat bottom of the pressure cooker with cooking spray. Set on heat or sauté. Add chicken, cook until chicken is no longer pink, stirring to break apart. Add pizza sauce, vegetables, and undrained tomatoes.

Cover and set the timer for 15 minutes. Release pressure manually.

Arrange split rolls, cut sides up, on a broiler pan. Broil 3 to 4 inches from the heat for 1 to 2 minutes or until toasted. Spoon mixture onto bottoms of toasted rolls. Top with cheese and roll tops. Makes 8 sandwiches.

Fennel and Pear Chicken Thighs

Ingredients

- 1 medium fennel bulb, trimmed and cut into
- 1/2-inch-thick wedges
- 2 6oz. jars (drained weight) sliced mushrooms
- 1/2 cup coarsely snipped dried pears
- 2 tbls. quick-cooking tapioca, finely ground
- 2 1/2 pounds skinless, boneless chicken thighs
- 3/4 teaspoon salt
- 1/2 teaspoon dried thyme, crushed
- 1/2 teaspoon cracked black pepper
- 1 cup pear nectar or apple juice
- Hot cooked couscous or rice

Procedure

Combine sliced fennel, mushrooms, and dried pears to the pressure cooker. Sprinkle with tapioca. Add chicken thighs; sprinkle with salt, thyme, and pepper. Pour pear nectar over mixture in cooker.

Cover and set timer for 12 minutes. Release pressure manually.

Serve chicken with hot cooked couscous. Makes 6 servings.

Pressure Cooker Turkey Chili

Ingredients

- 1 1/4 pounds lean ground turkey
- 1 large onion, chopped
- 1 garlic clove, minced
- 1 tablespoon olive oil
- 1 1/2 cups frozen corn kernels
- 1 red bell pepper, chopped
- 1 green bell pepper, chopped
- 1 (28-oz.) can crushed tomatoes
- 1 (15-oz.) can black beans, rinsed and drained
- 1 (8-oz.) can tomato sauce
- 1 (1.25-oz.) package chili seasoning mix
- 1/2 teaspoon salt
- Toppings: shredded Colby and Monterey Jack
- cheese blend, finely chopped red onion

Directions

Heat the oil in the pressure cooker in the heat or brown mode.

Add the onion and garlic and stir till lightly cooked, stirring until turkey crumbles and is no longer pink; drain.

Add all the rest of the ingredients (except the cheeses) and mix well.

Close and lock the lid and set the timer for 10 minutes.

Let the pressure reduce naturally. Serve with choice of toppings.

Beef Diablo

Ingredients

- 1 cup beef broth
- 4 lbs. pot roast, boneless
- 3 potatoes, peeled/sliced
- 1 onion sliced
- 2 tbs. flour
- 1 tbs. prepared mustard
- 1 tbs. chili sauce
- 1 tbs. Worcestershire sauce
- 1 tsp. vinegar
- 1 tsp. sugar

Directions

Trim all excess fat from roast. Add the beef broth to the pressure cooker.

Place potatoes and onion in bottom of the cooker. Make a smooth paste of flour, mustard, chili sauce, Worcestershire sauce, vinegar and sugar. Spread over top of roast. Place roast in the pressure cooker on top of potatoes and onions. Cut roast in half if necessary to fit in the pressure cooker. Cover and lock the lid and set the timer for 60 minutes. When the cooking time is done let the pressure reduce naturally. Remove roast from cooker to cutting board, let cool for 10 minutes then slice against the grain.

Chicken Santa Fe

Ingredients

- 1 cup chicken broth
- 1 (15 oz.) can black beans, rinsed and drained
- 2 (15 ounce) cans whole kernel corn, drained
- 1 cup bottled thick and chunky salsa, divided
- 5 or 6 skinless, boneless chicken breast halves
- 1 cup shredded Cheddar cheese

Directions

In the pressure cooker, mix together the beans, corn, chicken broth and 1/2 cup salsa.

Top with the chicken breasts, then pour the remaining 1/2 cup salsa over the chicken.

Cover and lock the lid and set the timer for 12 minutes. Seal the pressure valve.

When cooking time is done wait 10 minutes and then release the remaining pressure manually.

Maple Country Style Ribs

Ingredients

- 1 cup beef broth
- 1 1/2 lbs. country style
- pork ribs
- 1 tablespoon maple syrup
- 1 tablespoon soy sauce
- 2 tablespoons dried minced onion
- 1/4 teaspoon ground cinnamon
- 1/4 teaspoon ground ginger
- 1/4 teaspoon ground allspice
- 1/2 teaspoon garlic powder
- 1 dash ground black pepper

Directions

Mix together the maple syrup, soy sauce, minced onions, cinnamon, ginger, allspice, garlic powder and black pepper.

Cut the ribs into smaller sections and brush the mixture all over the ribs. Add the beef broth to the pressure cooker and add a rack or trivet.

Place the ribs on the rack, close and lock the lid

Set the timer for 20 minutes.

Release the pressure naturally, open the lid, remove ribs and serve.

Pressure Cooker Venison Roast

Ingredients

- 1/2 cup water
- 3 pounds boneless venison roast
- 1 large onion, sliced
- 1 tablespoon soy sauce
- 1 tablespoon Worcestershire sauce
- 1 tablespoon garlic salt
- 1/4 teaspoon ground black pepper
- 1 (1 ounce) package dry onion soup mix
- 1 (10.75 oz.) can of condensed cream of mushroom soup

Directions

Put cleaned meat in pressure cooker and cover with onion. Sprinkle with soy sauce, Worcestershire sauce, garlic salt and pepper.

In a small bowl combine the soup mix, water and the soup. Mix together and pour mixture over venison. Close and lock the lid and set the timer for 20 minutes.

Let the pressure reduce naturally.

Country Pork and Mushrooms

Ingredients

- ¼ cup water
- 2 lbs. country-style ribs, boneless
- 1 can cream of mushroom soup
- 4 oz. sliced mushrooms
- 1/4 tsp salt
- 1 envelope mushroom gravy mix
- 1/8 tsp pepper
- 1/2 tsp paprika

Directions

Combine all ingredients in the pressure cooker. Cover and lock the lid and set the timer for 15 minutes. Allow the pressure to release naturally.

Creole Dump

Ingredients

- 1 tablespoon olive oil
- 1/4 cup chopped onion
- 1/4 cup green bell pepper
- 1 clove minced garlic
- 1 (14 ounce) can whole tomatoes, chopped and undrained
- 2 teaspoons Worcestershire sauce
- 2 teaspoons red wine vinegar
- 1/2 teaspoon dried basil
- 1/4 teaspoon salt
- 1/4 teaspoon pepper
- 1/4 teaspoon pepper sauce (optional)
- 1 1/2 lbs. chicken pieces (4 to 6)

Directions

Put the chicken in the bottom of the pot. Pour remaining ingredients over the chicken. Close and lock the lid and set the timer for 10 minutes. Release the pressure manually.

Honey Ginger Dump Chicken

Ingredients

- 4 tablespoons chopped onion
- 2 tablespoons honey
- 1 tablespoon soy sauce
- 1 tablespoon minced ginger
- ½ cup sherry
- 1/4 cup chives
- 1 1/2 lbs. chicken pieces (boneless, skinless preferred)

Directions

Put the chicken in the bottom of the pot. Pour remaining ingredients over the chicken. Close the lid and set the timer for 10 minutes. When cooking is done wait 5 minutes and then release the remaining pressure manually.

Raspberry Currant Chicken

Ingredients

- 4 boneless chicken breasts (cut into bite sized pieces)
- 1 tablespoon Sugar
- 1 Teaspoon Pepper
- 1/8 cup Water
- 1/8 cup Raspberry Vinegar**
- 1/2 cup Currant Jelly

Directions

Place all the ingredients into the pressure cooker and mix to coat the chicken.

Close and lock the lid and set the timer for 10 minutes

Release the pressure manually, open lid and serve over rice

**(Also can substitute Raspberry Vinaigrette Salad Dressing for the vinegar)

Kielbasa Stew

Ingredients

- 1-1/2 lb. turkey kielbasa, cut into 1 in. pieces, low fat
- 2 lb. sauerkraut, rinsed and drained
- 3 Granny Smith apples, peeled, cored and cut crosswise into rings
- 1 onion, thinly sliced and separated into rings
- 2-1/2 lb. red potatoes, quartered
- 2 cups chicken stock
- 1/2 tsp caraway seed
- 1/2 cup shredded Swiss cheese

Directions

Place half the sausage in the pressure cooker and top with sauerkraut. Cover with remaining sausage, apple and onion. Top with potatoes. Add stock and sprinkle with caraway seeds. Cover lock the lid and set the timer for 15 minutes. When cooking is done wait 5 minutes then release the pressure manually.

Southwestern Chicken

Ingredients

- 2 (15 1/4 oz.) cans whole kernel corn, drained
- 1 (15 oz.) can black beans, rinsed and drained
- 1 (16 ounce) jar chunky salsa, divided
- 6 boneless skinless chicken breast halves
- 1 cup (4 ounce) shredded Cheddar cheese

Directions

Combine corn, black beans and 1/2 cup of the salsa in pressure cooker. Top with chicken; pour the remaining salsa over chicken.

And lock the lid and set the timer for 12 minutes.

Release the pressure manually and open.

Sprinkle with cheese; cover until cheese is melted - about 5 minutes.

Serves 4

Pressure Cooker Sichuan Beef & Carrots

Ingredients

- 1 1/2 lbs. boneless chuck roast, cut in cubes
- 1 cup carrots, cut lengthwise (approx 1/4-inch thick)
- 2 cloves garlic, crushed
- 1 tbs. brown sugar
- 1/2 tsp red pepper flakes
- 1/3 cup soy sauce
- 2 tbs. hoisin sauce
- 1/2 tsp dark sesame oil
- 1 1/2 cups water
- 1 tbs. olive oil for browning meat
- Thickening:
- 1 1/2 tbs. cornstarch
- 3 tbs. water
- Optional Topping:
- small red chili peppers
- sliced green onions

Directions

Heat oil in pressure cooker. When oil starts to shimmer, add meat and brown on all sides; remove from pan deglaze pan with the 1 1/2 cups water, scraping up all the browned bits on the bottom. Add the carrots and then the meat on top of the carrots.

Add the garlic, brown sugar, pepper flakes, soy sauce, hoisin sauce and dark sesame oil. Stir thoroughly then pour over the meat and carrots in the pressure cooker. Close and lock the lid and set the timer for

15 minutes. Let the pressure reduce naturally.

If you want to thicken the sauce–when meat and carrots are done, remove from the pressure cooker and keep warm. Set cooker to heat or simmer. Mix the cornstarch and water and stir into hot liquid, stirring until smooth. Simmer for about 5-10 minutes. Add the meat and carrots back to the gravy. Heat through and serve.

Serves about 4.

Beef and Mushrooms (with a secret ingredient)

Ingredients

- 1 1/2 lb. chuck roast, trimmed of any excess fat and cubed
- 2 Tbsp. flour
- 4 tsp regular bouillon
- 2 Tbsp. dried minced onion
- 1/2 tsp black pepper
- 8 oz. sliced mushrooms
- 1 tsp garlic powder
- 1/2 cup evaporated milk
- 1 Tbsp. quick cooking tapioca
- 1 Tbsp. Worcestershire sauce
- 1 Tbsp. tomato paste
- 1/2 cup lemon lime soda (like Sprite, not diet)
- Parsley, for garnish

Directions

Place cubed roast in pressure cooker. Sprinkle the flour over the meat and stir to coat.

Add in the bouillon, onion, pepper, mushrooms, garlic powder, evaporated milk, tapioca, Worcestershire sauce, tomato paste and soda. Stir to coat.

Cover and lock the lid and set the timer for 12 minutes. Let the pressure reduce naturally.

Remove lid and stir a bit. Serve beef, sauce and mushrooms over noodles or potatoes or rice. Top with parsley for garnish.

Beef Stroganoff

Ingredients

- 2 lbs. Stew Meat (sliced into bite-size pieces)
- 1 can or fresh Mushrooms (sliced as desired), optional
- 1 pkg. onion soup mix
- 1 (10 3/4 oz.) can Cream of Mushroom Soup
- 1 (12oz.) can Ginger Ale
- 1-2 Tbsp corn starch
- 1 (8 oz.) Sour Cream, *room temperature
- 1 pkg. *Egg Noodles

Directions

Place stew meat in pressure cooker

Add mushrooms, onion soup mix, cream of mushroom soup, and ginger ale and stir

Close and lock the lid and set the timer for 15 minutes

Release the pressure manually and open the lid.

Mix 1-2 Tablespoon of corn starch with a small amount of water and add to thicken

Add sour cream to taste (optional)

Cook egg noodles according to the package directions

Serve the stroganoff over *noodles and enjoy!

Apple Sauce BBQ Chicken

Ingredients

- 4 boneless skinless chicken breasts
- 1/2 t ground pepper
- 2/3 cup chunky applesauce
- 2/3 cup BBQ sauce (I used Brown Sugar/Hickory)
- 2 T brown sugar
- 1 t chili powder

Instructions

Place chicken breasts on bottom of the pressure cooker

Mix all remaining ingredients together, and pour over chicken.

Close and lock the lid and set the timer for 12 minutes

Release the pressure manually. Serves 4.

Pressure Cooker London Broil

Ingredients

- 1 1/2 pounds London broil
- 2 cloves garlic, minced
- 1 (10.75 ounce) can cream of mushroom soup
- 1/2 cup water
- 1/2 teaspoon dried basil
- 1/2 teaspoon dried oregano
- 1/2 teaspoon salt
- Add all ingredients to list

Directions

Place the London broil in pressure cooker; add the garlic, mushroom soup, water, basil, oregano, and salt; cover and lock the lid and set the timer for 20 minutes. When cooking time is done wait 5 minutes then release the pressure manually.

Orange Chicken with Potatoes

Ingredients:

- 8 chicken thighs skinless
- 1 tbsp. olive oil
- 1 tsp. kosher salt
- 1 tsp. pepper
- 1 small butternut squash, seeded, peeled and cut into 1" pieces
- 1 tsp. jarred minced garlic
- 1 orange cut into ¼" rings
- 1 onion, cut into eights
- 1 tsp. honey
- 8 sprigs thyme
- I cup low sodium chicken broth

Instructions:

Pat the chicken dry with a paper towel and season with salt and pepper. Set the pressure cooker on the heat, brown or sauté mode and add the oil. Brown the chicken on all sides, about 4 minutes per side.

Deglaze the cooker pan with the chicken broth, scrap off any brown bits from bottom. Add the remaining ingredients and close and lock the lid.

Set the timer for 10 minutes at high pressure. When done release the pressure manually.

Mediterranean Chicken with Olives & Tomatoes

Ingredients:

- 4 chicken leg quarters (about 3-4 lbs.}
- 1 tbsp. olive oil
- 1 tsp. kosher salt
- 1 tsp. pepper
- 1 small lemon
- ½ cup of cooking wine or white wine
- 1 cup pimiento-stuffed Spanish olives, halved
- ½ cup pitted Kalamata olives, halved
- 1 tsp. jarred minced garlic
- 1 (141/2-oz.) can diced tomatoes with basil, garlic and oregano undrained
- 1 Tbsp. fresh thyme
- 3 oz. feta cheese crumbled (optional)

Instructions:

Pat the chicken dry with a paper towel and season with salt and pepper. Set the pressure cooker to the brown, saute or heat mode and add the oil.

Add the chicken to the cooker (2 at a time) brown on all sides, about 4 minutes per side. Remove chicken to a plate after browned

Deglaze the cooker pan with the wine, scraping off any brown bits from the bottom. Grate, zest and squeeze 1 Tbsp. of juice from the lemon and 1 tsp. of grated zest.

Add the lemon juice and zest, the olives, thyme, garlic and tomatoes in a medium bowl. Add the chicken back to the cooker and pour the mixture over the chicken.

Close and lock the lid. Set the timer for 10 minutes at high pressure.

When the cooking time is up release the pressure manually and open the lid and serve.

Braised Chicken Thighs with Carrots and Potatoes

Ingredients:

- 1 ½ lb. chicken thighs skinless
- 1 lb. baby carrots
- 1 ¼ tsp. salt divided
- ¼ cup chicken broth
- ¼ cup dry white wine
- 1 tsp. jarred minced garlic
- ½ tsp. dried thyme
- 1 tsp. paprika
- 1/2 chopped red medium onion halved lengthwise and sliced
- 4 medium sized new potatoes (about 1 lb.) cut into ¼" thick slices.

Instructions:

Place the onions topped with the potatoes and carrots into the pressure cooker.

Combine the salt, pepper, broth, wine, garlic and thyme and pour mixture over vegetables. Combine paprika, salt, and pepper and rub over chicken thighs. Place chicken on veggies. Close and lock the lid. Set the timer for 10 minutes at high pressure.

When the cooking cycle is over and the beeper sounds release the pressure manually. Open the lid and serve the chicken over vegetables.

Creamy Cheesy Chicken Spaghetti

Serves: *4*

Ingredients

- 1 lb. boneless skinless chicken breasts (I used one really big one!)
- 1 shallot, chopped (about 2 tablespoons)
- 3 cloves minced garlic
- ¼ teaspoon salt
- ⅛ teaspoon pepper
- 3 cups chicken broth
- 16 oz spaghetti noodles, uncooked
- 8oz cream cheese
- 2 cups shredded cheese (I used a cheddar, colby, and monterey jack blend)

Instructions

Add the chicken breast, shallot, garlic, salt, pepper and broth to the pressure cooker

Cover and lock the lid. Set the timer for 10 minutes at high pressure.

When the cooking time is up release the pressure manually. Open the lid. Remove the chicken. Shred chicken breast and return to the pressure cooker.

Break uncooked noodles in half and add to the cooker along with cream cheese. Give it a stir and replace cover and set the timer for 10 more minutes.

When the cooking time is up wait 5 minutes then release the pressure and open the lid. Add the shredded cheeses and stir everything to combine and serve immediately

Mac and Cheese with Garlic Chicken

Serves: *4*

Ingredients

- 1 lb. boneless skinless chicken (I used breast tenders)
- 3 cups chicken broth
- 2 cloves minced garlic
- 1 teaspoon garlic powder
- ¼ teaspoon salt
- ⅛ teaspoon pepper
- 16 oz. pasta noodles (your favorite to use for mac and cheese)
- 12 oz. shredded cheese of choice (6 oz. each of sharp white and yellow cheddar)
- 4 oz. cream cheese

Instructions

Place the chicken in the pressure cooker and add broth, garlic, garlic powder, salt and pepper. Cover and lock the lid. Seal the pressure valve, and set the timer for 6 minutes at high pressure. When cooking time is up, do a quick release. Remove chicken from cooker and shred with two forks

Add the noodles, along with the shredded chicken, close the lid and set the timer for 10 more minutes. When the cooking time is up, release the pressure naturally and open the lid.

Add the cream cheese and mix, then add the white and yellow cheese and blend. Stir and serve

Chicken in Vodka Sauce

Serves: *4*

Ingredients:

- 1 jar Bertolli Vodka Sauce
- 4 skinless boneless chicken breast halves
- 1 box penne pasta

Instructions:

Put chicken in the pressure cooker pot. Pour the vodka sauce over chicken.

Close and lock the lid. Seal the pressure valve and set the timer for 10 minutes at high pressure. When the cooking time is up and the beeper sounds wait 5 minutes then release the pressure manually.

During the 10 minutes of cooking time boil the pasta and cook el dente. Serve chicken over penne pasta with a salad

Chicken Paprika

Serves: *4*

Ingredients

- 2.5 lbs. bone-in, skin-on chicken thighs
- 1 tsp. salt
- ¼ tsp. pepper
- 2 Tbsp. butter
- 1 large onion sliced
- 1 (14-oz.) can chicken broth
- 2 tsp. Hungarian sweet paprika
- ¾ cup sour cream (ADD THIS AT THE END)

For serving
- cooked egg noodles

Instructions

Sprinkle the chicken with the salt and pepper. Set the pressure cooker in the heat or brown mode and add the butter. When the pan is hot, brown the chicken on both sides, no need to cook through. Remove the chicken and set aside on a plate.

Add the onion, chicken broth and paprika to the pressure cooker and stir. Using tongs add the chicken into the paprika sauce.

Cover and lock the lid. Seal the pressure valve and set the timer for 10 minutes.

When the cooking time is through and the beeper sounds, release the pressure manually.

Remove the chicken on to a plate. Add enough egg noodles to the be submerged and slightly covered by the cooking liquid. Set on heat or sauté and simmer to a boil, mixing the noodles and cook till al dente. Add the sour cream to the sauce in the cooker and stir until it gets as smooth as possible.

Add the chicken back to the pressure cooker into the sauce. Serve over noodles and enjoy.

Apricot Russian Chicken

Serves: *4*

Ingredients

- 1 (12 oz.) jar of apricot preserves
- 1 (16 oz.) bottle of Russian salad dressing
- 4 boneless, skinless chicken breasts
- ½ onion, chopped
- ½ cup water

Instructions

Place chicken breasts inside the pressure cooker. (Browning optional)

In a bowl, mix half the jar of apricot preserves with 2 and ½ cups of Russian salad dressing and ½ cup of water

Stir in the chopped onions. Mix well. Pour the mixture over the chicken.

Close and lock the lid and set the timer for 10 minutes at high pressure.

When the cooking time is up and the beeper sounds, release the pressure manually. Serve over a pile of white rice, with a side of green beans.

Cranberry Chicken

Serves: *4*

Ingredients

- 4 boneless, skinless chicken breasts
- 1 cup French dressing
- 1 15-ounce can whole cranberry sauce, or 1 cup homemade cranberry sauce
- 1 pack dry onion soup mix
- ½ cup water

Instructions

Place chicken breasts in the bottom in a single layer. (Chicken can be browned first in the sauté mode- this is optional)

Whisk together French dressing and cranberry sauce and water. Pour over chicken. Turn chicken to coat all sides of the chicken.

Cover and lock the lid. Seal the pressure valve. Set timer for 10 minutes.

When the cooking time is up and the beeper sounds, release the pressure manually. Garnish with toasted pine nuts and chopped parsley if desired and serve.

Butter Chicken

. . . .

Serves: *4*

Ingredients

- 1 Tbsp. olive oil
- 2 lbs. boneless, skinless chicken breasts, cut into 1 inch pieces.
- 9 cloves garlic, crushed
- 1 (14 oz.) can light coconut milk
- 1 (6 oz.) can tomato paste
- 2 Tbsp. flour
- 2 tsp. garam masala
- ½ tsp. cayenne, or to taste
- 1 tsp. dried coriander
- 1 Tbsp. paprika
- 1 tsp. tumeric
- 1 tsp. cumin
- 1½ tsp Kosher salt, or to taste
- Freshly ground pepper to taste

Instructions

Heat the olive oil in the pressure cooker on the "heat or brown" setting. Add the chicken and cook until evenly browned.

Add the garlic and cook continuously stirring for about 1 minutes.

Stir in coconut milk, tomato paste, flour, garam masala, cayenne, coriander, paprika, tumeric, cumin, salt and pepper.

Stir and cook for about 2 min. until thoroughly mixed. Add in salt and pepper. Add in chicken, stir well. Cover lock the lid. Seal the pressure valve and set the timer for 10 minutes at high pressure.

When the cooking time is up and the beeper sounds release the pressure manually. Serve over rice and with naan bread if desired.

Chicken Parmesan

Serves: *6*

Ingredients

- 6 boneless, skinless chicken breasts
- 2 cups panko bread crumbs
- 2 large eggs, beaten
- 4 tbsp. olive oil, divided
- 1 (44-oz.) jar tomato-basil sauce
- ¾ tsp. salt
- ½ tsp. pepper
- 1 (8oz.) package of shredded mozzarella cheese
- ¾ cup shredded parmesan cheese
- 16 oz. cooked pasta

Insructions

Prepare 6 aluminum foil pieces (approx 12" x 12")

Pour breadcrumbs in a large bowl or plate. Dip chicken breasts one at a time in the egg. Place into the bread crumbs and coat both sides.

Heat 2 tbsp. of oil in the pressure cooker on the heat or sauté mode.

Cook the chicken breasts, two at a time for 2-5 minutes till browned on both sides. Remove each breast to a foil when each is done browning.

Spoon sauce over each breast then sprinkle on both cheeses. Fold foil around each chicken breast and seal to make a packet.

Add 1 ½ cups of water and a trivet to the pressure cooker. Place the packets on the trivet. Close and lock the lid. Seal the pressure valve. Set the timer for 10 minutes on high pressure. When the cooking time is up, release the pressure manually. Open the lid and carefully remove the packets, cut open and serve.

Hungarian Chicken with Smoked Paprika

Serves: *4-6*

Ingredients

- 3 lbs. skinless chicken pieces
- 1 cup chicken broth
- 1 red bell pepper, seeded and sliced
- 1 yellow bell pepper, seeded and sliced
- 1 onion, sliced
- 1 can of diced tomatoes (28 oz.)
- 1 garlic clove, minced
- 1 tsp. picante Spanish smoked paprika, or 1 ½ Hungarian paprika
- 2 tbsp. of olive oil
- 1 tbsp. kosher salt
- ½ tsp. pepper
- 1/3 cup sour cream
- Hot cooked pasta

Instructions

Sprinkle the chicken with salt and pepper. Heat the oil in the pressure cooker. Add the chicken and brown on all sides, about 8 minutes. Do it in 2 batches if necessary not to crowd the pot. Pour in ½ of the broth to deglaze the pan and scrape off any loose pieces from the bottom of pot.

Add the pepper, onion, garlic, tomatoes and the remaining broth. Close and lock the lid and seal the pressure valve. Set the timer for 10 minutes at high pressure. When the cooking time is up, release the pressure manually and open the lid. Remove the chicken with a slotted spoon or tongs. Separate the meat from the bones, discard the bones and return the meat to the pressure cooker. Stir in the sour crem and mix till blended. Serve Chicken over cooked pasta.

Spicy Lime Chicken

Serves: *3-4*

Ingredients

- 2½ pounds (or so) of chicken pieces with bones and skin (wings, drumsticks and thighs)
- 2 tablespoons butter
- 1 tablespoon olive oil
- ½ teaspoon dried thyme
- ¼ teaspoon salt
- ⅛ teaspoon pepper
- ¼ cup Sriracha sauce
- ¼ cup lime juice
- ¼ cup water
- 1-2 fresh limes (optional)

Instructions

Heat oil and butter in the pressure cooker on the heat or sauté mode. Season skin side of chicken with salt, pepper and thyme

Place skin side down in the cooker (working in batches if needed to make sure chicken has plenty of room to cook)

Let chicken cook for about 6 minutes until it gets a nice brown crust

Flip chicken and pour (or brush) with Sriracha

Let simmer an additional 3-4 minutes

Add lime juice and let it cook down for a minute or two turning chicken a couple times to coat

Add ½ cup water and top with fresh sliced limes if desired

Close and lock the lid. Seal the pressure valve. Set the timer for 10 minutes at high pressure. When the cooking time is up release the pressure manually. Open thevlid and serve.

Chicken Risotto PC

Ingredients

- 2 tablespoons olive oil
- 1 ½ lbs. chicken thigh fillets trimmed and cut into 2" pieces
- 1 onion, finely chopped
- 2 garlic cloves, finely chopped
- 1 ½ cups Arborio rice
- ½ cup dry white wine
- 3 ¼ cups chicken broth
- ¾ cups grated parmesan cheese
- ½ stick of butter, diced
- 3 oz. baby spinach

Instructions

Heat 1 tbsp. of the oil in the pressure cooker in the heat or sauté mode. Cook chicken in 2 batches for 3-5 minutes or until well browned. Heat the remaining oil and stir in the onion and cook until tender. Stir in the garlic and sauté till fragrant. Add the rice and stir until opaque. Return the chicken to the pressure cooker and add the stock and wine. Stir to combine. Close and lock the lid and seal the pressure valve. Set the timer for 7 minutes. When done release the pressure manually. Open the lid. Add the butter and cheese and let stand for 5 minutes then mix in the spinach.

Creamy Mushroom Chicken with Leeks

Ingredients

- 2 medium leeks, sliced
- 2 Tablespoons olive oil
- 6 boneless, skinless chicken breasts
- ¾ teaspoon salt, divided
- ¾ freshly ground pepper, divided
- ¼ cup whipping cream
- 1 tablespoon course-grianed mustard
- 5 garlic clove minced
- 1 can (101/2 oz.) cream of chicken soup
- ¼ cup water
- Hot cooked rice

Instructions

Sprinkle chicken with ½ of the salt and pepper on both sides

Heat the oil in the pressure cooker on the heat or sauté mode.

Add the chicken and brown in small batches (2 breasts at a time). When done and all the chicken is in the pressure cooker add the remaining salt and pepper, mustard, and garlic cloves. Pour the soup and water over the chicken.

Close and lock the lid and seal the pressure valve. Set the timer for 10 minutes at high pressure. When the cooking time is up wait 5 minutes, then release the pressure manualy. Open the lid and serve over rice.

Honey Garlic Chicken and Vegetables

Ingredients:

- 8 bone-in, skin-on chicken thighs
- 16 oz. baby red potatoes, halved
- 16 oz. baby carrots
- 16 oz. green beans, trimmed
- 2 tablespoons chopped fresh parsley leaves

For the sauce

- 1/2 cup reduced sodium soy sauce
- 1/2 cup honey
- 1/4 cup ketchup
- ¼ cup water
- 2 cloves garlic, minced
- 1 teaspoon dried basil
- 1/2 teaspoon dried oregano
- 1/4 teaspoon crushed red pepper flakes
- 1/4 teaspoon ground black pepper

Instructions:

In a large bowl, combine soy sauce, honey, ketchup, water, garlic, basil, oregano, red pepper flakes and pepper.

Place chicken thighs, potatoes, carrots and soy sauce mixture into the pressure cooker. Cover and lock the lid and seal the pressure valve. Set the timer for 10 minutes at high pressure. When the cooking time is up, release the pressure manually and open the lid. Add the green beans, secure the lid and seal the pressure valve. Set the timer for 3 minutes. When done release the pressure manually, open lid and serve the chicken with the vegetables.

Chicken Provencal

Ingredients

- 2 lbs. skinless chicken thighs, cut into quarters
- 2 medium red bell peppers, cut into ¼" thick slices
- 1 medium yellow bell pepper, cut into ¼" thick slices
- 1 onion, thinly sliced
- 1 can (28 oz.) plum tomatoes, drained
- 3 cloves garlic, minced
- ¼ teaspoon salt
- ¼ teaspoon dried thyme
- ¼ teaspoon ground fennel seed
- 3 strips orange peel
- ½ cup fresh basil leaves, chopped (optional)
- ½ cup water

Instructions

Pour in the tomatoes. Add the peppers, garlic, onions, orange peel and spices. Place the chicken breasts on top of all and seal the lid. Seal the pressure valve and set the timer for 10 minutes. When the cooking time is up, wait 5 minutes then release the pressure manually. Open the lid, serve.

Chicken and Sweet Potato Stew

....

Serves: *4*

Ingredients

- 4 boneless, skinless chicken breasts, cut into 1 inch pieces
- 2 medium sweet potatoes cubed
- 2 medium Yukon Gold potatoes, cubed
- 2 medium carrots, cut into ½-inch slices
- 1 can (28 ounces) whole stewed tomatoes
- 1 cup chicken broth
- 1 teaspoon salt
- 1 teaspoon paprika
- 1 teaspoon celery seeds
- ½ teaspoon black pepper
- 1/8 teaspoon ground cinnamon
- 1/8 teaspoon ground nutmeg

Directions

Comine all ingredients into the pressure cooker and stir. Close and lock the lid. Seal the pressure valve. Set the timer for 10 minutes at high pressure. When the cooking time is up wait 5 minutes then reduce the pressure manually. Open the lid and serve with slotted spoon.

Sesame Chicken with Vegetables

Ingredients

- 1 ½ pounds skinless boneless chicken breasts cut into 1" pieces
- 1 ¼ cups chicken broth
- ½ cup firmly packed brown sugar
- ¼ cup corn starch
- 2 Tbsp. rice vinegar
- 1 Tbsp. soy sauce
- 2 Tbsp. sweet chili sauce
- 2 Tbsp. honey
- 2 tsp. dark sesame oil
- 2 cups sugar snap peas
- 2 cups crinkle cut carrots
- 1 ½ Tbsp. toasted sesame seeds
- Hot cooked rice. Garnish – chopped green onions

Instructions

Mix together the first 8 ingredients in the pressure cooker. Add the chicken, pes and carrots. Stir all together well. Close and lock the lid. Seal the pressure valve and set the timer for 10 minutes. When the cooking time is up release the pressure manually. Open the lid. Mix ½ cup of the cooking broth with the corn starch and mix to a slurry. Pour slurry into the pressure cooker and mix till thickened.

Pressure Cooked Angel Chicken

Serves: *4*

Ingredients

- 2-4 boneless chicken breasts
- 1 packet dry Italian dressing mix
- 4 oz cream cheese
- 3 Tbsp. butter
- 1 can Cream of Chicken
- 3/4 cup chicken broth or white wine
- Angel hair pasta, cooked

Directions

Place chicken in pressure cooker. Combine all remaining ingredients except pasta. Pour over chicken. Close and lock the lid and seal the pressure valve. Set the timer for 10 minutes at high pressure.

When the cooking time is up wait 5 minutes and then release the pressure manually (quick release). Open the lid and serve over cooked angel hair pasta.

Pressure Cooker Shredded Chicken

Ingredients

- 2 pounds chicken - boneless & skinless
- ½ cup zesty Italian dressing
- ½ tablespoon minced garlic (I use more like a full tablespoon)
- ½ tablespoon chili powder
- ½ tablespoon ground cumin
- 1 (1 oz) packet Ranch Dressing Mix (mix with ½ cup water)

Instructions

Place all your ingredients except for the chicken into your pressure cooker and stir. Sprinkle the chicken with salt and pepper and add to the pessure cooker.

Close and lock the lid and seal the pressure valve. Set the timer for 10 minutes. When the cook time is up release the pressure manually then open the lid. Remove the chicken to a cutting board and shred using 2 forks.

Put the shredded chicken back into the pressure cooker and mix with the left over juices. Serve in salads, tacos, burritos ect.

Stupid Easy Chicken

Ingredients

- 4 skinless boneless chicken breasts
- 1 (28-ounce) can Italian-seasoned diced tomatoes
- 1 envelope Herb and Garlic Recipe soup mix (Lipton's or similar)
- hot cooked rice or pasta
- Parmesan cheese, grated

Instructions

Cut chicken into bite-size pieces. Mix chicken, tomatoes and soup mix together, and pour into pressure cooker.

Close and lock the lid and seal the pressure valve. Set the timer for 8 minutes.

When the cooking time is up, wait 5 minutes then release the pressure manually. Open the lid. Serve over rice or bow tie pasta and sprinkle with Parmesan cheese.

Coconut Curry Chicken

Serves: *6*

Ingredients

- 2 pounds skinless, boneless chicken breasts, cut into cubes
- 2 potatoes, peeled and cubed
- 1 onion chopped
- 1 garlic clove minced
- 1 (13.5oz.) can coconut milk
- 1 cup chicken broth
- 1/4 cup curry powder
- 1/4 teaspoon fresh ground pepper
- 1 red beel pepper, cored and chopped
- 1 tablespoon cornstarch
- 1 tablespoon raisins, or to taste
- 1 tablespoon flaked coconut, or to taste

Instructions

Place chicken, potatoes, onion, garlic, coconut milk, chicken broth, curry powder, salt, and black pepper in a slow cooker.

Mix the coconut milk, chicken broth, curry powder, salt and pepper together and pour into the pressure cooker.

Add the potatoes, onion and garlic and chicken and stir all together

Close and lock the lid and seal the pressure valve. Set the timer for 10 minutes on high pressure.

When the cooking time is up wait 5 minutes then release the pressure manually. Open the lid and stir in the bell pepper.

Stir in the cornstarch and simmer for 5-10 minutes or until thickened, sprinkle with raisins and coconut flakes then serve.

Quick Pressure Cooker BBQ Chicken

Ingredients:

- 4 boneless, skinless chicken breasts or thighs (about 2 lbs. total)
- 2 cups favorite salsa
- salt and pepper
- ¼ cup water
- (optional: fresh lime wedges for serving)

Instructions:

Sprinkle the chicken breast with salt and pepper. Add the water to the pressure cooker. Place chicken breasts in the pressure cooker and cover with salsa. Toss until covered. Secure the lid. Seal the pressure valve. Set the timer for 10 minutes at high pressure. When the cooking time is up release the pressure manually and open the lid.

Remove the chicken to a cutting board and shred with two forks. Add back to cooker.

Mix chicken back into the salsa and juices and let simmer for a few minutes, then serve. Makes great sandwich.

Lemon Butter Chicken

Ingredients:

- 8 bone-in, skin-on chicken thighs
- 1 tablespoon smoked paprika
- Kosher salt and freshly ground black pepper, to taste
- 3 tablespoons unsalted butter, divided
- 3 cloves garlic, minced
- 1 cup chicken broth
- 1/2 cup heavy cream
- 1/4 cup freshly grated Parmesan
- Juice of 1 lemon
- 1 teaspoon dried thyme
- 2 cups baby spinach, chopped

Instructions

Season chicken thighs with paprika, salt and pepper, to taste.

Melt 2 tablespoons butter the pressure cooker on the heat or sauté mode. Add chicken, skin-side down, in batches and sear both sides until golden brown, about 4-5 minutes per side; drain excess fat and set aside.

Add the remaining tablespoon of butter to the cooker. Add the garlic, stirring frequently, until fragrant, about 1-2 minutes. Stir in the chicken broth and return the chicken to the cooker. Add the lemon juice and thyme.

Close and lock the lid and seal the pressure valve. Set the timer for 12 minutes. When the cooking time is up release the pressure manually (quick release). Open the lid. Set the pressure cooker to the heat or sauté mode, bring to a boil and add the heavy cream. Add the spinach and simmer till wilted and the sauce thickens a bit. Serve immediately.

Pressure Cooker General Tsao's Chicken

Ingredients

- ■ 4 boneless, skinless chicken breasts cut into 1" pieces
- ■ 1/2 cup water
- ■ 3 Tablespoons hoisin sauce
- ■ 2 Tablespoons soy sauce
- ■ 1/2 cup brown sugar
- ■ 3 Tablespoon ketchup
- ■ 1/4 tsp dry ginger
- ■ 1/2 tsp crushed red pepper (more or less to liking)
- ■ 1 Tablespoon cornstarch

Directions

Mix together water, hoisin sauce, soy sauce, brown sugar, ketchup, ginger, and crushed red pepper in a medium sized bowl.

Add the chicken to the pressure cooker and pour the sauce over the chicken Close and lock the lid and seal the pressure valve. Set the timer for 8 minutes. When the cooking cycle is done let sit for 5 minutes and then release the pressure. Open the lid and check the thickness of the sauce. If you need to thicken the sauce

Set the pressure cooker to heat or sauté. Add 2 tablespoons of the hot cooking liquid to the cornstarch and mix till smooth. Pour the slurry into the pot and stir continuously while the cooker heats and the sauce thickens. When it is at it's desired consistency serve immediately over rice.

Herbed Chicken and Mushrooms

Ingredients:

- 3 pounds chicken thighs and/or drumsticks, skinned
- 1 tablespoon oil
- 5 cups sliced assorted fresh mushrooms. Shiitake, button, crimini, and/or oyster
- 1 red onion, cut into wedges
- 1/2 cup chopped carrot (1 medium)
- 1/4 cup dried tomato pieces (not oil-packed)
- 3/4 cup chicken broth
- 1/4 cup dry white wine or chicken broth
- 3 tablespoons cornstarch
- 1 teaspoon dried thyme, crushed
- 1/2 teaspoon garlic salt
- 1/2 teaspoon dried basil, crushed
- 1/4 teaspoon ground black pepper
- 4 1/2 cups hot cooked plain and/or spinach linguine or fettuccine, or hot cooked rice.

Instructions

Heat the oil in the pressure cooker in the heat or sauté mode. Add the chicken in batches to avoid crowding the pot. Cook first batch for 3-4 minutes on each side then do the remaining batches. Set chicken aside on a platter. Add the onions and carrots and sauté for 3-4 minutes. Add the tomatoes, mushrooms, chicken broth and wine, add back the chicken and stir. Sprinkle in the spices and close and lock the lid. Seal the pressure valve and set the timer for 10 minutes. When the cooking time is up release the pressure manually. Open the lid and stir. To thicken the sauce, take ½ a cup of the cooking liquid from the pot and mix in with the cornstarch to make a smooth slurry. Set the pressure cooker on heat and pour in the slurry. Stir continuously for about 5 minutes and then let simmer till thickened. Serve over pasta or rice.

Tomato Chicken with Vegetables

Ingredients

- 2lbs. bones skinless chicken breasts, cut to 1" strips
- 12oz. bag of mix vegetables (broccoli, carrots, cauliflower
- ½ jar of your favorite marinara sauce
- 1 tablespoon Adobo seasoning

Insructions

Add the tomato sauce to the pressure cooker then add the chicken and mix.

Sprinkle with adobo seasoning. Lock and close the lid and seal the pressure valve.

Set the timer for 5 minutes at high pressure. When cooking time is up do a quick release.

Open the lid and pour in the bag of vegetables. Close the lid and set the timer for 4 minutes.

When time is done release the pressure manually, open the lid and serve

Chicken Spinach Roll

Serves: *2-4*

Ingredients

- 2 boneless skinless chicken breasts
- 1 cup baby spinach
- ½ cup sliced and chopped mushrooms
- ½ cup tomato sauce
- 1 tsp. olive oil

Instructions

Prepare 2 pieces of aluminum foil (12" x12") Spread the oil in the center of each foil.

Flatten the chicken breasts with a meat mallet. Place one chicken breast on each foil.

Spoon a thin layer of tomato sauce on each tops with a handful of baby spinach. Sprinkle on some sliced chopped mushrooms and add a ½ tsp. olive oil.

Roll up the chicken in the foil, carefully keeping the content inside the rolled chicken. Seal the edges of the foil packet. Add one cup of water and a trivet or steam basket. Place the packets on the trivet and close and lock the lid. Seal the pressure valve.

Set the timer for 12 minutes at high pressure. When done wait 5 minutes then release the pressure manually.

Open the lid and remove the packets. Open the packets and remove the chicken roll and slice. Serve with additional tomato sauce spooned over the chicken

Healthy Chicken with Vegetables

Ingredients

- 4 Boneless, skinless chicken breasts
- 1 jar of tomato sauce (I use Mario Vitalie's natural marinara sauce)
- 2 cups broccoli florets
- ½ medium sized cauliflower, chopped
- 2 cups baby spinach
- 1 cup chopped kale
- ¼ cup water

Instructions

Add the sauce and the water to the pressure cooker.

Dump in the broccoli and cauliflower and mix contents well. Sprinkle the chicken breasts with salt and pepper.

Add the chicken on top of the vegetables in the pressure cooker.

Close and lock the lid and seal the pressure valve. Set the timer for 8 minutes.

When the cooking time is up wait 5 minutes then release the pressure manually. Open the lid and remove the chicken to a platter.

Add the spinach and kale. Stir till softened. Serve the chicken with the vegetables.

Pressure Cooked Korean Beef

Ingredients:

- 1 cup beef broth
- 1/2 cup reduced sodium soy sauce
- 1/2 cup brown sugar, packed
- 4 cloves garlic, minced
- 1 tablespoon sesame oil
- 1 tablespoon rice wine vinegar
- 1 tablespoon freshly grated ginger
- 1 teaspoon Sriracha, or more, to taste
- 1/2 teaspoon onion powder
- 1/2 teaspoon white pepper
- 3 pounds boneless beef chuck roast, cut into 1-inch cubes
- 2 tablespoons cornstarch
- 1 teaspoon sesame seeds
- 2 green onions, thinly sliced

Directions:

In a large bowl, Mix together beef broth, soy sauce, brown sugar, garlic, sesame oil, rice wine vinegar, ginger, Sriracha, onion powder and white pepper.

Place chuck roast the pressure cooker. Stir in the beef broth mixture until well combined. Close and lock the lid and seal the pressure valve. Set the timer for 25 minutes on high pressure. When the cooking time is up, release the pressure manually. Open the lid and serve, garnished with green onions and sesame seeds if desired

Savory London Broil

Serves: *4*

Ingredients

- 1 (2 lbs. Beef Steak Top Round London Broil
- 10.75 ounce) can condensed cream of mushroom soup
- 1 (10.75 ounce) can condensed tomato soup
- 1/2 cup water
- 1 (1 ounce) package dry onion soup mix

Instructions

Place meat in the bottom of the slow cooker; if necessary, slice meat to make it fit!

In a medium bowl, mix together water, mushroom and tomato soups. Pour mixture over beef. Sprinkle dry onion soup mix over top.

Cover and lock the lid. Seal the pressure valve. Set the timer for 30 minuteson high pressure. Open the lid and remove meat, let cool for 5-10 minutes then slice and serve. Spoon sauce over the meat.

Hawaiian Spareribs

Serves: *4*

Ingredients

- 1/4 cup vinegar
- 1/2 cup ketchup
- 2 tablespoons cornstarch
- 1/2 teaspoon salt
- 1/2 tablespoon fresh ginger, grated (optional)
- 3 lbs. pork spareribs, cut into serving size pieces
- 1 tablespoon soy sauce
- 1 (8 ounce) can crushed pineapple, undrained
- 3 tablespoons brown sugar
- 1/2 cup water

Instructions

Stir together the vinegar, ketchup, soy sauce, and pineapple. Stir in brown sugar, salt, and ginger.

Add ½ cup of water to the mixture. Add a layer of ribs and then pour on half the mixture.

Add the remaining ribs and pour over the rest of the mixture.

Close and lock the lid and seal the pressure valve. Set the timer for 25 minutes at high pressure.

When the cooking time is up wait 10 minutes then release the remaining pressure manually.

Open the lid and set the cooker to heat or sauté. Remove the ribs to a platter using tongs.

Stir in the cornstarch and simmer till the sauce thickens. Serve the ribs and spoon over sauce.

Pressure Cooker Roast Beef with Coffee

Ingredient

- 3 lbs. chuck roasts
- 5 garlic cloves, peeled
- 1½ cups fresh brewed strong coffee
- Tablespoons of cornstarch
- 1cup water
- 1 teaspoon of salt
- 1 teaspoon of pepper

Instructions

Place the roast on a cutting board, sprinkle with salt & pepper make 5 slits all around the meat.

Push a garlic clove into each slit, make sure it goes in deep. Place the roast in the pressure cooker and pour in the coffee.

Close and lock the lid.

Seal the pressure valve and set the timer for 40 minutes.

When the time expires do natural release. Open the lid.

Remove to a platter. Shred the beef using 2 forks to pull apart

Serve in sandwiches or plate.

If you want to use the cooking juices for gravy, mix the cornstarch and water till smooth.

Set the cooker to heat and slowly mix in the cornstarch slurry mixing frequently for 5 minutes.

Simmer to boil if necessary to thicken the sauce. Serve over the beef.

Easy Beef Burgundy

Ingredients

- 1 ½ pounds cubed beef stew meat
- 1 can (10 ¾ ounces) condensed cream of mushroom soup
- 1 cup dry red wine
- 1 onion, chopped
- 4 ounces sliced mushrooms
- 1 1ounce package dry onion soup mix
- 1 tablespoon minced garlic
- 2 tablespoons olive oil
- Hot cooked noodles (optional)

Instructions

Heat the oil in the pressure cooker in the heat or sauté mode. Brown the beef on all sides. Add all the rest of the ingredients and stir. Close and lock the lid and seal the pressure valve. Set the timer for 20 minutes at high pressure. When the cooking time is done wait 5 minutes then release the pressure manually.

Sweet and Sour Brisket Stew

Ingredients

- 1 beef brisket (about 1 ½ lbs), trimmed and cut to 1" cubes
- 1 jar (12oz.) chili sauce
- 2 carrots cut into cut into ½" slices
- 1 onion, chopped
- ½ cup chicken broth
- 1 ½ tablespoons packed dark brown sugar
- 1 ½ tablespoons of lemon juice
- 1 teaspoon Dijon mustard
- 1 clove garlic, minced
- ¼ teaspoon paprika
- ½ teaspoon salt
- ¼ teaspoon black pepper

Directions

Combine the beef and all the rest of the ingredients into the pressure cooker. Close and lock the lid. Seal the pressure valve. Set the timer for 20 minutes at high pressure. When the cooking time is up release the pressure manually.

Swedish Meatballs

Serves: *6*

Ingredients:

- 1 (32 oz.) package fully cooked meatballs (thawed)
- 1 Tbsp. vegetable oil
- 1 tsp. salt
- 2 cups chicken broth
- 1/4 tsp. garlic powder
- ¼ cup all-purpose flour
- ¼ tsp. fresh ground pepper
- 1/8 tsp. ground nutmeg
- Tbsp. chopped fresh parsley
- ½ cup sour cream
- 1/2 cup white wine
- ½ cup red currant jelly (optional}

Instructions

Heat the olive oil in the pressure cooker on the "heat or brown" setting. Add the chicken and cook until evenly browned.

Cook the meatballs in batches for about 5 minutes, turning until browned on all sides. When all browned add all the meatballs back into the pressure cooker. Add the wine then the chicken broth and all the spices. Close and lock the lid. Seal the pressure valve and set the timer for 5 minutes. When the cooking time is up release the pressure manually. Open the lid and press the heat button. Remove the meatballs from the cooker with a slotted spoon and place in a serving bowl. Spoon out ¼ cup of the cooking liquid and mix with the flour till it turns to a smooth mixture. Stir the mixture back into the pressure cooker mixing well. Add the sour cream, parsley and jelly if desired and whisk well while simmering. Serve over cooked noodles.

Pressure Cooker Cranberry Corned Beef

Ingredients

- 3-4 lb. cured corned beef brisket with spice pack
- 5 large carrots, cut into 3" pieces
- 1 large onion cut into 6 wedges
- 1 (14oz.) can whole berry cranberry sauce
- 1 (14oz.) jellied cranberry sauce
- 2 (1oz.) envelope dry onion soup mix
- ½ cup beef broth
- ½ cup sour cream
- 4 tsp. refrigerated horseradish
- ¼ tsp. freshly ground pepper
- Garnish – chopped fresh parsley
- 1 tablespoon extra-virgin olive oil

Instructions

Trim the fat from the brisket. Sprinkle the spice pack on both sides. Heat the oil in the pressure cooker on the heat or sauté mode. Brown all sides of the brisket (If too big to fit in cooker, cut in half). Remove the brisket to a plate and add the beef broth to deglaze. Place the carrots and onions in and place the brisket on top.

Combine the cranberry sauces and soup mix and spoon over brisket

Close and lock the lid and seal the pressure valve. Set the timer for 40 minutes at high pressure. Meanwhile combine the horseradish and sour cream in a small bowl. Cover and chill till ready to serve.

When done let the pressure release naturally. Open the lid and remove the brisket to a platter. Spoon carrots and onions and a little cooking liquid around the brisket on the platter. Stir the pepper into the horseradish mix and serve with sauce.

Pressure Cooker Beef with Olives

Ingredients

- ¼ cup melted butter
- 3 lbs. boneless top sirloin steak, cut into 1 ½ inch pieces
- ¼ tsp. salt
- ½ tsp. pepper
- 1 tbsp. olive oil
- 3 large garlic cloves, sliced
- 2 shallots, vertically sliced
- 2 cups pimiento-stuffed Spanish olives
- 2 Tbsps. olive juice from jar
- (12oz). jar roasted bell peppers, drained and cut to thick strips
- ½ cup beef broth

Instructions

Heat the oil in the pressure cooker in the heat or sauté mode. Cook the beef in 2 batches, about 2 minutes on each side.

Add the garlic and shallots and sauté for 1 minute, mixing in with the beef. Add the broth. Coarsely chop

I cup olives and sprinkle chopped and whole olives and the olive juice over the beef.

Close and lock the lid and seal the pressure valve. Set the timer for 15 minutes at high pressure. When the cooking time is up, release the pressure manually. Open the lid and add in the bell peppers just before serving.

Pepper Steak with Mushrooms

Ingredients

- 1 ½ lb. top round steak cut diagonally across the grain into thin slices
- 1 tsp. salt, divided
- ½ tsp. pepper, divided
- 1 Tbsp. vegetable oil
- 3 cups green. red and yellow precut pepper mix
- 2 garlic cloves, minced
- 1 medium onion, vertically sliced
- 1 (14oz.) can diced tomato with basil, garlic and oregano
- 1 (8oz.) sliced baby portabella mushrooms
- 1 (10 ½-ounce) can beef consommé
- 2 Tbsp. soy sauce
- 2 Tbsp. tomato paste
- 2 Tbsp. cornstarch

Instructions

Sprinkle the beef with half of the salt and half of the pepper.

Heat the oil in the pressure cooker on the heat or sauté mode. When oil is hot add beef. Cook beef till browned on both sides (6-8 minutes). Add the bell peppers'

Mix in the garlic, onion, tomatoes and mushrooms into the cooker and toss gently. Whisk together the consommé, soy sauce, tomato paste, salt and pepper and stir in. Close and lock the lid and seal the pressure valve. Set the timer for 25 minutes. When the cooking time is up release the pressure manually. Open the lid.

Mix together the cornstarch and 2 Tbsp. water, slowly stir into liquid in the cooker.

Set on heat, simmer and stir until the sauce thickens. Good served over rice or mashed potatoes.

Pressure Cooker Cowboy Pot Roast

Ingredients

- 1(2 ½-3lb) eye of round roast, trimmed
- 1 ½ tsp. salt
- 1 ½ tsp. pepper
- 1 (14.5oz.) can petite-cut diced tomatoes, drained
- 1 (10oz.) can diced tomatoes and green chiles, undrained
- 1 onion cut into 8 wedges
- 1 tbsp. chili powder
- 2 tbsp. of vegetable oil
- 2 (16oz,) can pinto beans, drained
- 1 (15oz.) can of black beans, drained

Instructions

Combine 1 tsp. salt, 1 tsp. pepper, and 2 cans of diced tomatoes in a medium bowl. Sprinkle the roast with the remaining salt and pepper.

Heat the oil in the pressure cooker on the heat or sauté mode.

Brown the roast on all sides in the hot oil. Pour the tomato mixture over the roast. Close and lock the lid and seal the pressure valve. Set the timer for 40 minutes. When the cooking time is up release the pressure manually. Open the lid.

Remove the roast and cut into large chunks. (keep warm)

Mash 1 ½ cans of pinto beans and add to the cooker, stir until combined. Stir in the black beans and the remaining ½ can pinto beans.

Add the roast pieces back into the pressure cooker and close and lock the lid.

Seal the pressure valve and set the timer for 5 minutes. When done release pressure

Manually. Open the lid and serve.

Garlic Stuffed Roast

Ingredients:

- 2 pounds beef chuck roast
- 12 cloves garlic peeled cut into quarters and sliced
- salt and pepper
- handful fresh oregano sprigs
- 8 ounces tomato sauce
- 1 cup water

Instructions:

Cut deep slits (12) all over the roast (both sides and ends). Put the garlic cloves into the slits. Sprinkle the roast with salt and pepper.

Lay half the sliced onions and oregano sprigs over the bottom of the pressure cooker. Place the roast on top, and spread remaining onions and oregano over the roast.

Pour the tomato sauce over the roast, and pour the water around the meat. Cover and lock the lid and seal the pressure valve.

Set the timer for 35 minutes. When the cooking time is done do a natural release.

Open the lid, remove the oregano sprigs and remove the meat to a platter, cut and serve.

Pressure Cooker Marriage Meatloaf

Ingredients

- 2 pounds ground beef
- ¾ cups quick oats, uncooked
- 2 well-beaten eggs
- ¼ cup chopped onion
- ¾ cup tomato juice
- 2 teaspoons salt
- 1½ teaspoons pepper

Sauce:

- 2 tablespoons ketchup
- 2 tablespoons mustard
- 2 tablespoons brown sugar

Instructions

Combine all meatloaf ingredients thoroughly.

Pack firmly into a loaf pan that fits inside the pressure cooker. Mix together sauce ingredients and spread over meatloaf.

Place a rack or trivet into the pressure cooker and add 1 cup water.

Make a sling out of aluminum foil around the baking pan to make it easier to remove. Loosely cover the top of the loaf pan with aluminum foil and place on the trivet.

Close and lock the lid and seal the pressure valve. Set the timer for 25 minutes at high pressure. When the cooking time is up let the pressure release naturally. Open the lid and remove pan.

Stupid Easy Wicked Beef and Noodles

Ingredients:

- 1 1/2 pounds ground beef
- 1/2 teaspoon salt
- 1/2 teaspoon garlic powder
- 1 jar Alfredo sauce
- 1/2 can diced tomatoes and chilies (use more, if desired)
- 1 box (16oz.) elbow or macaroni of your choice – cooked
- 1 tbsp. vegetable oil
- Pinch of red pepper flakes

Instructions

Prepare pasta according to package directions.

While pasta is cooking, heat the oil in the pressure cooker in the heat or sauté mode.

Add the ground beef and cook till separated and browned. Add salt and garlic powder. Drain and set aside. Mix together the Alfredo sauce and the diced tomatoes and add the mixture to the pressure cooker. Add

the beef and mix to coat. Close and lock the lid and seal the pressure valve.

Set the timer for 15 minutes. When the cooking time is done, release the pressure manually. Open the lid. Strain the pasta and add it to the pressure cooker. Mix well and serve.

Stir in red pepper flakes to taste.

Cherry Glazed Beef Roast

Ingredients

- 2.5 pound round roast
- ¼ cup stone ground mustard
- 2 teaspoons dried rosemary
- ¼ cup balsamic vinegar
- 10 oz cherry preserves
- ½ cup beef broth
- 1 cup frozen cherries
- ¼ cup water
- 1 Tbsp. oil

Instructions

Rub the roast on all sides with mustard and rosemary.

Heat the oil in the pressure cooker in the heat or sauté mode.

Add the meat and brown the roast on each side for about 3-4 minutes or until lightly browned

Deglaze pan with balsamic vinegar.

Add beef broth and frozen cherries to slow cooker and spread cherry preserves over top of the roast. Close and lock the lid. Seal the pressure vale and set the timer for 40 minutes.

When the cooking time is up, let the pressure release naturally. Open the lid, remove the roast, slice and serve.

Honey Garlic Beef with Veggies

Ingredients:

- 2 lbs. cubed stew meat
- 16 ounces baby red potatoes, halved
- 16 ounces baby carrots
- 16 ounces green beans, trimmed
- 2 tablespoons chopped fresh parsley leaves

For the sauce

- 1/2 cup reduced sodium soy sauce
- 1/2 cup honey
- 1/4 cup ketchup
- 2 cloves garlic, minced
- 1 teaspoon dried basil
- 1/2 teaspoon dried oregano
- 1/4 teaspoon crushed red pepper flakes
- 1/4 teaspoon ground black pepper
- ¼ cup water

Instructions

Combine soy sauce, honey, ketchup, water, garlic, basil, oregano, red pepper flakes and pepper in a large bowl.

Place the meat and the soy sauce mixture into the pressure cooker. Cover and lock the lid and seal the pressure valve. Set the timer for 15 minutes. When the cooking time is up release the pressure manually. Open the lid and add the potatoes, carrots and green beans. Reseal the lid and the pressure valve and set the timer for 10 minutes. When the cooking time is up let the pressure release naturally. Open the lid and serve the beef with the veggies.

Portuguese Madeira Beef Shanks

Serves: *4*

Ingredients

- 4 medium beef shanks, bone in (about 3 pounds)
- 1 cup beef broth
- 1 cup dry Madeira wine
- 1 large onion, chopped
- 1 green bell pepper diced
- ½ cup diced celery
- ½ cup fresh minced Italian parsley
- 2 jalapeno peppers, seeded and minced
- 4 garlic cloves minced
- 1 tablespoon fresh rosemary, minced
- 1 teaspoon salt
- Hot cooked rice (optional)

Instructions

Add the beef shanks to the pressure cooker, then pour in the beef broth and wine over the shanks. Add all the rest of the ingredients and stir the shanks.

Close and lock the lid. Seal the pressure valve. Set the timer for 30 minutes at high pressure. When the cooking time is done let the pressure release naturally. When pressure is released open the lid, carefully remove the shanks (the meat will be falling off the bone)

Serve over rice and spoon the sauce on top.

Mushroom Beef

Ingredients

- 1 1/2 lb. boneless beef sirloin tip steak, or stew beef cut into 1-inch pieces
- 1 jar (12 oz.) beef gravy
- ¼ cup water
- 1 tablespoon Worcestershire sauce
- 1 tablespoon spicy brown mustard
- 2 cans mushrooms (4 ounces each), drained
- 2 tablespoons all-purpose flour
- 2 tablespoons water

Instructions:

Add the beef, beef gravy, Worcestershire sauce, mustard, water and mushrooms to the pressure cooker

Cover and lock the lid. Seal the pressure valve and set the timer for 30 minutes. When cooking time is up release pressure manually.

In small bowl, mix flour and water; stir into beef mixture. Set cooker to heat or sauté and simmer until thickened.

Spoon beef and mushroom mixture over potatoes, noodles, or rice.

Pressure Cooker Swiss Steak

Ingredients

- 5 bacon slices, haved
- 8oz. pre-chopped celery, onion and bell pepper mix
- 2 Tbsp. jarred minced garlic
- 1 ¼ ib. round steak, about 1" thick. Cut into 4 equal portions
- 1/3 cup all-purpose flour
- 1 ½ teaspoons salt
- ¾ tsp. ground pepper
- 2 cups beef broth
- 1 (14 ½ -oz.) can diced fire roasted tomatoes1 Tbsp. Worcestershire sauce
- 1 tsp. dried Italian seasoning
- 1 tablespoon oil

Directions

Heat the oil in the pressure cooker in the heat or sauté mode.

Cook the bacon in the pressure cooker for 5-6 minutes or until crisp. Remove bacon. Crumble and set aside. Add the celery and garlic in the left over oil, stirring until tender, then remove.

Place the meat on a sheet of plastic wrap and flatten with a meat mallet until it is about ¼" thick. Combine the flour, salt and pepper in a shallow bowl and dredge the meat in the flower. Cook the chicken in the cooker till browned on both sides. Remove the chicken and add back the vegetables then add back the chicken over the vegetables. Add the remaining ingredients and pour the beef broth over the beef.

Close and lock the lid and seal the pressure valve. Set the timer for 15 minutes, When the cooking time is up, release the pressure manually. Open the lid and serve.

Light Beer London Broil

Ingredients

- 1 ½ lbs. London broil
- 1 tablespoon olive oil
- 1 teaspoon butter
- ½ medium sized onion chopped
- 1 12oz. bottle of lite beer
- 1 small can of tomato paste
- 2 teaspoons salt
- 1 teaspoons pepper

Directions

Heat the oil and butter in the pressure cooker in the heat or sauté mode.

Add the onions and sauté till translucent, about 5 minutes. Add the London broil and brown on both sides. Add the tomato paste and a half the beer and mix together till smooth. Pour the remaining beer over the meat. Cover and lock the lid and seal the pressure valve. Set the timer for 20 minutes at high pressure. When the cooking time is done, release the pressure manually. Open the lid and remove the meat to a cutting board. The are 3 things you can do at this point.

1 Slice and serve with spooned cooking sauce from the cooker.

2 Slice very thin slices and use for delicious steak sandwiches.

3 Shred the meat with 2 forks, return to the cooker and simmer for 5 minute the serve.

Creamy Honey Mustard Pork Chops

Ingredients

- 2 Tbs. olive oil
- 3 Tbs. honey
- 2 Tbs. Dijon mustard
- 1 ½ lbs. pork chops, thin, boneless
- 2 Tbs. cream
- 1 tsp lemon juice, fresh
- 2 tsp corn flour
- 1 cup water
- Salt & pepper to serve

Instructions

Heat 1 tablespoon of oil in the pressure cooker in the heat or sauté mode. Add the pork chops and brown on both sides. Remove and set aside.

Add 1 cup of water to the pressure cooker and add a trivet or rack. Mix the oil, honey, cream, lemon juice and mustard in a small bowl. Make a slurry with the corn flour and 2 tablespoons of hot water and Wisk till smooth and thick. Spread it all over each side of every chop and place them on the rack in the cooker. Close and lock the lid and seal the pressure valve. Set the timer for 15 minutes at high pressure. When the cooking time is up release the pressure manually. Open the lid and serve with rice or pasta. Spoon on remaining sauce.

Brown Sugar Pork Chops

Serves: *6*

Ingredients

- 2 tablespoons extra virgin olive oil
- 4 pounds boneless center cut pork chops, about 1-inch thick
- 1 teaspoon salt
- 1/2 teaspoon freshly ground pepper
- 12 ounces frozen orange juice concentrate, thawed
- 1 cup packed brown sugar
- 3 tablespoons soy sauce
- 4 garlic cloves, peeled and smashed
- 2 large onions, thickly sliced
- 1/4 cup cornstarch
- 3 tablespoons water

Instructions

Sprinkle the pork chops with salt and pepper on both sides.

Heat the oil in the pressure cooker in the brown or saute mode. Brown pork chops on both sides. Work in batches, using remaining olive oil as necessary. Set aside.

Place the sliced onion and garlic in the pressure cooker.

Whisk together orange juice concentrate, brown sugar and soy sauce in a bowl.

Place 6 pork chops on top of onions and garlic in the cooker. Pour half of the orange juice mixture over the pork chops. Layer with remaining pork chops and pour remaining sauce over.

Close and lock the lid and seal the pressure valve. Set the timer for 15 minutes at high pressure. When the cooking time is done release the pressure manually. Open the lid and set the pressure cooker to heat. Add a slurry of the cornstarch and water and mix it into the cooking liquid stirring until the sauce thickens.

Coconut Shredded Pork

Ingredients

- 3-4 lb butt roast (bone in is all the better)
- 2 teaspoon salt
- ½ teaspoon red pepper flakes
- 1 teaspoon ground ginger
- 2 teaspoons garlic powder, or 2 cloves crushed
- 2 teaspoons chinese five spice
- ¼ teaspoon black pepper
- 2 teaspoons onion powder
- 1¾ cup or 1 13.5 oz. can full fat coconut milk
- 1 tablespoon fish sauce

Instructions

Mix together the salt, pepper flakes, garlic, five spice, pepper and onion powder. Sprinkle on all sides of the pork. Put the meat in the pressure cooker

Pour the can of coconut milk over the pork. Spread the cream over the the top of the pork.

Close and lock the lid and seal the pressure valve. Set the timer for 40 minutes at high pressure. When the cooking time is done release the pressure naturally

When the pressure is released remove the pork and set aside. Strain the fat from the broth that is in the crock pot into a in the pressure cooker and simmer for about 15 minutes.

While that is going remove fat and bone from the roast and shred the meat. Stir the pork into the sauce and serve.

Hearty Pork Stew

Serves: *6-8*

Ingredients

- 2 lbs. sweet potatoes, peeled and cut into ½" pieces (about 2 cups)
- 2 lbs. boneless pork shoulder roast, cut into 1" pieces
- 1 (14.5 oz.) can of chicken gravy
- 1 teaspoon dried thyme leaves, crushed
- ½ teaspoon of crushed red pepper
- 1 can (15oz.) black eyed peas, rinsed and drained
- ½ cup water

Instructions

Place the potatoes in the pressure cooker and top with the pork pieces. Mix the gravy, water, thyme, peas and red pepper in a bowl.

Pour mixture over the pork and potatoes.

Close and lock the lid and seal the pressure valve. Set the timer for 15 minutes at high pressure.

When the cooking time is up let the pressure release naturally.

Peach Glazed Pork Chops

Ingredients

- 4-6 boneless pork loin chops (about 1.5 pounds)
- 2 tablespoons butter
- 1 cup peach preserves (no sugar added)
- ½ teaspoon thyme
- ½ teaspoon salt
- ¼ cup water

Instructions

Heat the butter in the pressure cooker in the heat or sauté mode

Add the pork chops and brown on both sides (2 at a time) Mix the peach preserves with the water till smooth

With all the chops in the pressure cooker pour sauce over them

Cover and lock the lid and seal the pressure valve. Set the timer for 15 minutes. When the cooking time is up allow the pressure to release naturally

Open the lid, remove the chops to a plate and spoon over left over sauce.

Breaded Pork Chops

Serves: *4-6*

Ingredients

- 1 cup crushed corn flake crumbs
- 5-6 pork chops, ¾ inch thick
- 1 egg, beaten
- 1 tablespoon milk
- 3 tablespoons oil
- 1 cup water
- Salt and pepper

Instructions

Season pork chops with salt and pepper then dip in egg combined with milk. Dredge through the corn flakes to coat on both sides.

Heat the pressure cooker and add the oil.

Brown chops on both sides and remove. Add a trivet to the cooker. Add water; place pork cops on trivet and close cover securely.

Seal the pressure valve and set the timer for 15 minutes at high pressure. When the cooking time is done let the pressure release naturally.

Thai Pork with Peppers

Serves: *4*

Ingredients

- 1 lb. boneless pork chops
- 1 cup chicken broth
- 1/3 cup soy sauce
- 1/3 cup creamy peanut butter
- 3 tablespoons honey
- 6 cloves garlic, minced
- 2 tablespoons minced fresh ginger root
- 1 teaspoon crushed red pepper flakes
- 2 red bell peppers, thinly sliced and cut into bite-size lengths

Directions

Place the chicken broth, soy sauce, peanut butter, honey, garlic, ginger, crushed red pepper flakes, red bell peppers, and pork chops into the pressure cooker, stir together.

Close and lock the lid. Seal the pressure valve. Set the timer for 20 minutes at high pressure. When the cooking time is up, release the pressure manually. Remove the pork from the sauce. Shred the pork and return to the sauce. Let simmer for 5 minutes and serve.

Onion/Apple Pork Butt

Serves: *4-6*

Ingredients

- 3 lb pork butt
- 2 medium onions cut into chunks
- 2 cups of apple juice

Instructions

Place pork butt in the pressure cooker. Add all the onion chunks around pork butt. Pour in the apple juice. Sprinkle with pepper. Close and lock the lid.

Make sure the pressure valve is sealed and set the timer for 40 minutes high pressure. When the cooking time is up, release the pressure manually. Open the lid.

Remove the pork to a cutting board and shred or slice.

Veal Chops with Figs

Serves: *4*

Ingredients

- 1 cup pomegranate juice
- ¾ cup sugar
- 6 garlic cloves, minced
- 1 Tbsp. chopped fresh thyme
- 1 tsp. ground pepper
- 4 veal rib chops (1 to 1 ½ inches thick)
- 1 Tbsp. olive oil
- 2 shallots, vertically sliced
- 1 (8 oz.) package of dried figs, coarsely chopped
- 1 Tbsp. balsamic vinegar
- Fresh thyme for garnish

Instructions

Combine the garlic, thyme, and pepper and rub over veal. Heat the oil in the pressure cooker in the heat or sauté mode.

Brown veal 2 minutes on each side and remove to a plate. Add shallots and stir for 2 minutes.

Add the pomegranate juice, sugar and ½ cup of water, mix and let simmer for 5 minutes. Add the veal and spoon the figs on top. Drizzle with vinegar.

Close and lock the lid. Seal the pressure valve and set the timer for 25 minutes at high pressure. When the cooking time is done, release the pressure manually. Open the lid and serve.

Fruited Lamb Tagine

Serves: *2-4*

Ingredients

- 2 lbs. boneless leg of lamb cut into 1" cubes
- 2 Tbsps. All-purpose flour
- 2 tsp. garam marsala
- ½ tsp. ground turmeric
- 1 tsp. salt
- 1 tsp. pepper
- 2 Tbsp. olive oil
- 8 oz. prechopped onion
- 2 cups beef broth
- 1 cup dried pitted plums
- 1 cup diced apricots
- ½ cup orange marmalade
- Toasted almonds, chopped fresh cilantro for garnish

Instructions

Combine the flour, masala, turmeric, salt and pepper in a large zip lock bag. Add and seal the bag and shake to coat.

Heat the oil in the pressure cooker in the heat or sauté mode. Add the lamb (in batches if necessary so as not to crowd the pan) and cook for 2 minutes on each side or until pieces are browned. Add the onion and the broth, plums, apricots and marmalade. Stir well and close and lock the lid.

Seal the pressure valve. Set the timer for 20 minutes at high pressure. When the cooking time is up, release the pressure manually. Open the lid and serve. Good served over couscous.

Braised Rosemary Lamb Chops

Serves: *4*

Ingredients:

- 4 lamb shoulder chops
- 1 tbs. olive oil
- 1 tsp. salt
- 4 tsp. Greek seasoning
- 1 8 oz. mixture of chopped onions, celery and bell pepper
- 1 cup chicken broth
- ¼ cup chopped drained sundried tomatoes in oil
- 1 tsp. chopped fresh rosemary
- ¼ tsp. chili powder
- 1 (16 oz. can garbanzo beans, drained
- 1 (14 oz. can artichoke hearts, drained
- Hot cooked couscous
- Toasted pine nuts

Instructions:

Heat the olive oil in the pressure cooker on the "heat or brown" setting.

Season the lamb chops with Greek seasoning and place in the pressure cooker. Cook for 3 minutes on each side or until browned. Remove chops.

Add celery mix and cook for 2 minutes. Add chicken broth, stirring to loosen brown bits. Add the beans and the artichokes. Place the lamb chops back into the cooker

Mix in the sun-dried tomatoes, rosemary and chili powder.

Close and lock the lid. Seal the pressure valve. set the timer for 35 minutes at high pressure.

When the cooking cycle is done and the beeper sounds wait 5 minutes then do a quick release. Spoon the lamb and vegetables over couscous and sprinkle with pine nuts.

Spicy Sweet Potato Soup

Ingredients

- 3-4 large sweet potatoes, peeled and chopped into 1 inch pieces (or packages precut)
- 1 can chipotle peppers in adobe sauce
- 1 onion, diced
- 1 garlic clove, chopped
- ¼ tsp black pepper
- ¼ tsp salt
- 1 tsp cumin
- 6 cups vegetable or chicken broth
- ½ cup whole milk
- ¼ cup sour cream for garnish, optional

Instructions

Add sweet potatoes, chilis, onion, garlic, pepper, salt, cumin, and broth into the pressure cooker. Close and lock the lid and seal the pressure valve. Set the time for 15 minutes on high pressure.

When the cooking time is up let the pressure release naturally. Open the lid and stir. Check the thickness. If needed, use an immersion blender or transfer to a stand blender and blend mixture till smooth.

And the milk and mix or blend to combine.

Serve in individual bowls, garnished with a little sour cream if desired.

Healthy Summer Soup

Ingredients:

- 1 1/4 lbs. boneless skinless chicken breasts cut into bite sized pieces
- 1 1/4 cups chopped yellow onion (1 medium onion)
- 1 cup chopped celery (about 3 stalks)
- 4 cloves garlic, minced
- 2 Tbsp. extra virgin olive oil
- 3/4 cup dry quinoa
- 1/2 tsp dried thyme
- 1/2 tsp dried rosemary, crushed
- 4 (14.5 oz.) cans low-sodium chicken broth (7 cups)
- Salt and freshly ground black pepper, to taste
- 1 (15.5 oz) can Great Northern or Cannellini beans, drained and rinsed
- 4 cups packed kale, roughly chopped (thick ribs chopped and discarded)
- 3 Tbsp. chopped fresh parsley
- 2 Tbsp. fresh lemon juice
- Finely shredded parmesan cheese, for serving.

Directions:

Season the chicken with salt and pepper. Add the chicken broth and the quinoa to the pressure cooker. Drizzle with olive oil.

Add the chicken then the onions, celery and garlic. thyme, and rosemary

Cover and lock the lid and seal the pressure valve. Set the timer for 8 minutes at high pressure. When the cooking time is up, release the pressure manually. Open the lid.

Add in beans, kale, parsley and lemon juice, then cover, seal the pressure valve and set the timer for 5 minutes.

When done let the pressure release naturally. Serve warm topped with parmesan cheese.

Pressure Cooker Root Vegetable Soup

Ingredients:

- 1 large white onion, chopped
- 1 lb. butternut squash, peeled, seeded and chopped or pre-cubed
- 1 lb. carrots, peeled and chopped or baby carrots
- 1lb. parsnips, peeled and chopped
- 1 lb. sweet potatoes, peeled and chopped or pre-cubed
- 1 lb. Yukon Gold potatoes, peeled and chopped
- 2 celery ribs, stems removed and chopped
- 6 cloves garlic, peeled and thinly sliced
- 3 cups chicken or vegetable broth
- 1 bay leaf
- 1 Tbsp. fresh sage leaves, finely chopped
- 1 tsp. freshly ground black pepper
- 1/2 tsp. sea salt
- 2 cups chopped fresh kale

Instructions:

Add all the ingredients except the kale in the pressure cooker, and carefully stir to combine. Close and lock the lid and seal the pressure valve. Set the timer for 20 minutes. When the cooking time is up let the pressure release naturally and open the lid. Remove the bay leaf. Add the kale with the cooker on warm or sauté. Stir well and let simmer till the kale is softened. When the kale is softened remove and serve. Top with Parmesan cheese if desired.

Summer Vegetable Stew

Ingredients

- 1 cup vegetable broth
- 1 can (15oz.) chickpeas, rinsed and drained
- 1 medium zucchini, cut into ½" pieces
- 1 summer squash, cut into ½" pieces
- 4 large plum tomatoes cut into ½" pieces
- 1 cup frozen corn
- 1 teaspoon dried rosemary
- ¼ cup grated Asiago or Parmesan cheese (optional)
- 1 teaspoon chopped Italian parsley (optional)

Instructions

Pour the vegetable broth into the pressure cooker, followed by the chickpeas, zucchini, squash, plum tomatoes, corn and rosemary and mix well. Close and lock the lid.

Seal the pressure valve and set the timer for 15 minutes at high pressure. When the cooking time is up release the pressure manually. Open the lid and serve with cheese and parsley if desired.

Easy Risotto

Serves: *6*

Ingredients

- 1-2 tablespoon olive oil
- 1 medium onion, finely chopped
- 1 $\frac{1}{2}$ cups arborio rice
- 3 $\frac{1}{2}$ cups chicken stock
- black pepper, to taste
- 1-3 tablespoon romano cheese or 1-3 tablespoon parmesan cheese, for topping

Instructions

Heat oil in the pressure cooker. Add onion and sauté until translucent. Add rice and stock. Lock lid in place. Seal the pressure valve.

Set the timer for 8 minutes.

When the cooking cycle is done, release pressure naturally and open the lid.

Add black pepper to taste and 1 - 3 tbs. romano or parmesan cheese, also to taste. Serve immediately.

Fettuccine with Parsley Butter

Serves: *2*

Ingredients

- 2 tablespoons olive oil
- ½ lb. fettuccine pasta
- 3 cups chicken broth
- 1 teaspoon salt
- ¼ teaspoon white pepper
- ½ teaspoon dried summer savory,
- ¼ crushed cup butter, softened
- ¼ cup fresh parsley, chopped
- ¼ cup grated parmesan cheese

Instructions

In the pressure cooker, heat the oil. Stir fettucine into hot oil. Add broth, sa⸱ ⸱epper, and savory. Secure lid.

Set the timer for 8 minutes at HIGH PRESSURE. When Rem⸱⸱⸱ ⸱⸱n fettucine through a colander and return to the pressure cooker. Add butter and parsley, ⸱ ⸱⸱⸱⸱⸱ y until fettuccine is well coated. Pour into a serving bowl. Sprinkle with cheese.

Orange Rosemary Poached Salmon

Serves: *4*

Ingredients:

- 4 (6 oz.) skinless Salmon filets (1/2 to ¾" thick)
- 1 cup vegetable broth
- 1/2 cup fresh parsley leaves
- 3 teaspoon butter
- 6 garlic cloves pressed
- 2 5" sprigs of fresh rosemary
- 1 navel orange, sliced
- 1 tsp. orange zest
- 1 tsp. salt
- 1 tsp. ground red pepper
- 1 tsp. ground black pepper
- 1 cup orange juice

Instructions:

Sprinkle the salmon with orange zest, salt and peppers. Cover and chill.

Add the remaining ingredients into the pressure cooker. Add the chilled salmon. Close and lock the lid. Seal the pressure valve

Set the timer for 4-5 minutes. When the cooking time is up release pressure manually. Open the lid and transfer the salmon to a serving platter.

Greek Snapper

Serves: *4*

Ingredients

- 1 ½ cups white dry wine
- 1 thinly sliced onion
- 3 garlic cloves, minced
- (6 oz.) red snapper fillet (1" thick)
- 1 plum tomato chopped
- 1 tsp. dried oregano
- ½ tsp. salt
- ½ tsp. ground pepper
- 1 Tbsp. olive oil
- 1 oz. crumbled feta cheese
- Lemon wedges and fresh oregano for garnish

Instructions

Combine the first 4 ingredients into the pressure cooker

Close and lock the lid. Seal the pressure valve. Set the timer for 5 minutes at high pressure. When the cooking time is up release the pressure manually. Open the lid and add a trivet. Add the fish on the trivet in the pressure cooker.

Combine the tomato, oregano, salt & pepper in a bowl and spoon over fish. Drizzle oil over fish. Close and lock the lid. Set the timer for 5 minutes. Release the pressure manually when done.

Carefully remove the fish. Serve over rice. Spoon the tomato mixture over the fish. Sprinkle with feta cheese and serve with the lemon wedges.

Ginger Shrimp and Scallops Soup

Serves: *2*

Ingredients:

- 4 cups chicken broth
- ¼ lbs. uncooked shrimp
- ¼ lbs. raw scallops
- 2 Portobello mushrooms, sliced
- 1 cup sliced shitake mushrooms
- ½ cup sliced ginger root
- ½ cup chopped green onion
- ¼ cup chopped cilantro

Instructions:

Combine the stock and ginger in the pressure cooker. Cover and lock the lid. Seal the pressure valve. Set timer for 10 minutes, high pressure. When the cooking time is up release the pressure manually. Open the lid. Spoon the ginger out of the pressure cooker and add the mushrooms, shrimp, scallops and green onions. Close and lock the lid and seal the pressure valve. Set the timer for 5 additional minutes. When the time is up release the pressure manually. Open the lid and stir in the cilantro and green onions just before serving. (If shrimp and scallops are not cooked thru let simmer for 3 additional minutes.

Pressure Cooker Dijon Salmon

Ingredients

- 1/4 cup butter, melted
- 1 ½ tablespoons honey
- ¼ cups dry bread crumbs
- ¼ cup finely chopped pecans
- 3 tablespoons of Dijon mustard
- 3 teaspoons finely chopped fresh parsley
- 4 (4 ounces) Salmon Filet
- 1 tablespoon of olive oil
- Salt and pepper for seasoning

Instructions

Mix together in a bowl the mustard, honey and melted butter.

In another bowl mix together the bread crumbs, pecans and parsley.

Prepare 4 sheets of 12" x 12" sheets of auminum foil. Coat the middle of each with oil. Place a fillet on each sheet and spoon on the mushroom honey to cover.

Cover each piece with the breadcrumb mixture. Spray with can of butter or oil spray. Fold the foil around each piece and seal all the edges well but not to tight.

Put a trivet in the pressure cooker and pour in one cup water. Place packets on trivet

Close and lock the lid and seal the pressure valve. Set the timer for 6 minutes.

If you use low pressure set the timer for 8 minutes. When done, do a quick release. Remoe foil packs to a platter with tongs, slice open packets and eat from there or plate.

Simple PC Salmon

Ingredients

- 4 pieces' salmon (6oz) each
- 1 tablespoon of garlic
- ½ teaspoon of salt
- 2 tablespoons of butter
- 4 lemon wedges

Instructions

Preprare 4 12'x 12' sheets of aluminium foil.

Add a rack or trivet in the pressure cooker.and add a cup of water

Dap the center of each foil with olive oil and add the fillets to the foil.

Mix the garlic and salt in melted butter and pour over each fillet equally.

Top each with lemon slice then carefully fold the wrap and seal the corners.

Close and lock the lid and seal the pressure valve. Set the timer for 4 minutes.

When the cooking time is done, release the pressure manually andv serve.

Caribbean Shrimp with Rice

Serves: *2-4*

Ingredients

- 1 package (12 oz.) medium frozen shrimp thawed
- ½ cup chicken broth
- 1 garlic clove, minced
- 1 teaspoon chili powder
- ½ teaspoon salt
- ½ teaspoon dried oregano
- 1 cup frozen peas, thawed
- ½ cup diced tomatoes
- 2 cups cooked long grain rice

Instructions

Combine all ingredients except the shrimp into the pressure cooker.

Close and lock the lid. Seal the pressure valve. Set the timer for 5 minutes. When the cooking time is done, release the pressure manually and open the lid. Add the shrimp, stir and let simmer for 3-5 minutes.

Spoon shrimp and sauce over rice.

Pressure Cooker Eye of Round Roast with Gravy

Serves: *4*

Ingredients

- 1 (10 ounce) can cream of mushroom soup, undiluted
- 1 (10 ounce) can low sodium beef broth
- 1 (1 ounce) package dry onion soup mix (I use the onion-mushroom flavor)
- 1-2 tablespoon fresh minced garlic
- 1 tablespoon Worcestershire sauce
- 1 (3 lb.) eye of round roast
- ¼ cup flour
- 1 teaspoon black pepper
- ½-1 teaspoon garlic powder (optional)
- 3-4 tablespoons oil

Instructions

In a large bowl combine the mushroom soup with beef broth, dry onion soup mix, fresh garlic and

Worcestershire sauce; mix until combined,

In a small bowl mix together flour with black pepper and garlic powder (if using). Dredge the roast in the flour/black pepper mixture.

Heat oil in the pressure cooker; add in the roast and lightly brown on all sides. Pour the mixture over the roast. Secure the lid and set timer for 40 minutes When the cooking time is done release the pressure naturally. Open the lid.

For a thicker gravy, after cooking remove the roast and thicken with water/ cornstarch mixture.

Pressure Cooked Pot Roast with Creamy Gravy

Serves: *6*

Ingredients

- 3 lbs. chuck roast (or use your favorite cut)
- 1 teaspoon seasoning salt
- 1 teaspoon garlic powder
- 1 teaspoon ground oregano
- 1 teaspoon ground black pepper
- 1 1/2 ounces onion soup mix (use just ONE envelope)
- 1 (10 3/4 ounce) can condensed golden mushroom soup
- ½ cup water
- 2 tablespoons flour
- 2 tablespoons butter

Instructions

In a small bowl mix together seasoned salt, garlic powder, oregano, and onion soup mix. Rub mixture into all sides of roast, place into the pressure cooker

Spread golden mushroom soup over roast and pour in the water.

Close and lock the lid and set the timer for 40 minutes at high pressure. When the cooking time is up let the pressure release naturally. Open the lid. Remove the roast to a platter and cover with foil and let set for 10 minutes. Add 2 tablespoons of the roast liquid to the flour and make a paste.

Add the butter and the paste slowly while stirring till thickened. Slice the meat and serve with gravy.

Pressure Cooker Poached Salmon

Serves: *4 to 6*

Instructions

- 1 cup water
- 1 cup dry white wine
- 1 lemon, thinly sliced
- 1 shallot, thinly sliced
- 1 bay leaf
- 5-6 sprigs fresh herbs, (dill, and/or Italian parsley)
- 1 teaspoon black peppercorns
- 1 teaspoon kosher salt
- 2 pounds skin-on salmon (or 4-6 fillets)
- Kosher salt and freshly ground black pepper
- Lemon wedges, coarse sea salt, and olive oil for serving

Instructions

Place a rack or trivet in the pressure cooker. Season the top of the salmon with salt and pepper and place in the pressure cooker, skin side down. Put the lemon slices on top.

Pour the water, wine, shallots, bay leaf, herbs, peppercorns and salt over the fish in the pressure cooker. Close and lock the lid and seal the pressure valve. Set the time for 8 minutes at low pressure or 5 minutes

high pressure. When the cooking time is done release the pressure manually (quick release).

Open the lid and check the doneness. The salmon should be opaque and flake gently with a fork. If not to your liking cover the cooker and set the timer for another 5 minutes. When done drizzle on some extra virgin olive oil and sprinkle with sea salt or kosher salt. Serve with lemon wedges.

Vegetarian Minestrone

Ingredients

- 6 cups vegetable broth
- 1 (28 ounce) can crushed tomatoes
- 1 (15 ounce) can kidney beans, drained
- 1 large onion, chopped
- 2 ribs celery, diced
- 2 large carrots, diced
- 1 cup green beans
- 1 small zucchini
- 3 cloves garlic, minced
- 1 tablespoon minced fresh parsley
- 1 1/2 teaspoons dried oregano
- 1 teaspoon salt
- 3/4 teaspoon dried thyme
- 1/4 teaspoon freshly ground black pepper
- 1/2 cup of elbow macaroni
- 4 cups chopped spinach
- 1/2 cup of Shredded Parmesan cheese

Instructions

Combine vegetable broth, tomatoes, kidney beans, onion, celery, carrots, green beans, zucchini, garlic, parsley, oregano, salt, thyme, and black pepper in a 6-quart electric pressure cooker.

Close and lock the lid. Seal the pressure valve. Set the timer for 12 minutes.

When the cooking time is up, release the pressure manually and open the lid.

Add the elbow macaroni, stir and close and lock the lid. Set the timer for 6 minutes.

When the cooking time is up release the pressure manually, open the lid and stir in the spinach till softened.

To serve ladle into soup bowls and top with Parmesan cheese

Pepsi Pork Roast

Ingredients

- 3 lbs pork shoulder butt
- 1 (12 ounce) can Pepsi
- 1 (10 3/4 ounce) can cream of mushroom soup
- (1 1/4 ounce) package onion soup mix
- 1/2 cup corn starch

Instructions

Place roast in the pressure cooker

Mix soup mix with soup.

Add cola to soup mixture and pour over roast.

Close and lock the lid and seal the pressure valve. Set the timer for 30 minutes.

When done, open the lid and remove roast to a cutting board or platter and slice thinnley or shredd with 2 forks.

Remove a 1/2 cup of juices from the cooker and mix with the corn starch till smooth. Stir back to into the cooker.

Simmer and thicken juices with cornstarch for wonderful gravy.

Made in the USA
Middletown, DE
30 October 2016